My Journey with Phil

A Creative Perspective of Physical Reality

C.C. Stoner

BALBOA.
PRESS
A DIVISION OF HAY HOUSE

Balboa Press books may be ordered through booksellers or by contacting:

Balboa Press
A Division of Hay House
1663 Liberty Drive
Bloomington, IN 47403
www.balboapress.com
1 (877) 407-4847

Print information available on the last page.

ISBN: 978-1-5043-6142-2 (sc)
ISBN: 978-1-5043-6143-9 (e)

Balboa Press rev. date: 09/21/2016

Prologue

They say a journey begins with just one step. And so mine did. As I left a local diner with my coffee, I stepped into one of those balmy, fragrant winter nights for which South Florida is so famous. Foregoing my usual fashion of rushing from one activity to another I took a deep breath and eased into the sensual delights of the night.

How had I been so oblivious to the beauty and clarity of this perfect evening in my rush to grab a cup of coffee? I smiled in happy anticipation of returning to the Silva Method workshop I had been taking for the past three nights. There was a soft, humming feeling of expectation running through me, no doubt caused by the relaxation exercises I was learning from the Silva program. Little did I realize that in less than a minute, life as I knew it, would be forever and profoundly changed. Unaware, I had begun my journey.

Walking through the parking lot toward the street, I was amused to find that my over active mind was uncharacteristically tranquil; definitely beneficial to me. As a type A personality, I had been advised by my doctor to learn stress management before I ruined my health. The reason for taking this Silva Method workshop was to learn how to lighten up; to release my habitual, uptight dash into my day's agenda.

My daily schedule was crammed with home, children, graduate school and volunteer work. Needless to say this caused a great deal of stress, often expressed by painful muscles spasms. And now I had chosen to take this workshop right in the middle of mid-term exams.

As I approached the end of the parking lot, ready to cross the busy thoroughfare of Federal Highway, I paused to allow the traffic to clear. I looked into the bright lights of the approaching traffic and felt a perplexing shift in my immediate surroundings and within me. The air felt different, sweeter; my body tingled. I didn't seem to be breathing air but something more comforting. A strange word to use but nevertheless, the air filling my lungs felt comforting.

A calm, complete and profound, infused me. My senses expanded to a razor-sharp clarity I had never before experienced and I become intensely aware of everything at once and yet experienced each thing individually and completely. The smells of the citrus and Jasmine Florida night, the fragrant coffee, the feel of the hot styrofoam cup in my hands, the whisper of soft night air on my face, the fabric of my clothes on my skin, the sounds of the city, the chirping of the night insects, all of these sensations thrilled and elevated me to an astonishing awareness.

I looked up into the clear night sky and marveled at its beauty. Time ceased to exist and I understood the perfection of everything; God's handiwork, how it all fit together in the most simple, and yet amazing, intricate pattern; a perfect dance of creativity and manifestation and how necessary a component of that pattern mankind is. I felt my spirit lift and merge with the heavens, a peaceful and loving Oneness radiating around and through me. *I am blessed* filled my thoughts.

After some timeless duration, I became aware of another shift, moving, speeding, but beyond even the sense of velocity and I was swept into it. I felt an urgency to get back to class.

Now, I must get back now.

As I looked at the street I had to cross I was stunned to find I could not discern the individual lights of the on-coming cars. All traffic was whizzing along as one solid, buzzing mass; a monstrous stream of light and sound without interruption. I had a fleeting notion that the pupils of my eyes must be dilated. My body began to tremble. My heart was galloping in my chest, my breathing constricted, a full blown panic attack. My thoughts were a jumble of uncontrolled fears which exploded in my mind.

What is happening! Something is wrong with my eyes! Am I going blind? Am I having a heart attack? I'm all alone out here. I need help!

It was such a cruel and jarring departure from the profound peace I had just experienced. My mind was racing with insistent, fearful questions - *am I going to die here by the side of the road? I have to cross the street. I have to get back to the workshop. How will I ever get across this street?*

In the midst of my panic I heard, just to the right of me, a soothing, well modulated voice reply, "Don't worry. You'll get there."

I quickly turned to my right in monumental relief to thank my rescuer. But there was no one there. There was not a soul in that whole parking lot but me. I must have turned around in circles half a dozen times, looking for the person who had spoken to me. No one was there. No one.

Scared and utterly bewildered, I shouted into the night, "What is going on?"

Time shifted yet again and slipped into slow motion. Now I seemed to be the only thing moving in a static reality. I crossed that street in a state of amazement, totally unaware of the traffic or anything else. Somewhere between the street and the classroom, I felt renewed, no longer the person I was or would ever be again. That profound peace descended on me once more and I seemed to float along, not even feeling my feet touch ground as I returned to the workshop. From that moment I knew I was safe, loved and blessed.

When I walked into the classroom our instructor was just calling the class back to business. I smiled in wonderment that my experience had taken less than a fifteen minute coffee break. I felt as if I had been gone for a lifetime.

Light headed and giddy, I gazed at the faces of my fellow workshop attendees as they turned to welcome me back into the classroom. There appeared to be a glow about their smiling faces I had not noticed before I left for break. Actually, everything had a soft glow about it. Our instructor, Paul, was shining out loud. Everyone was so beautiful; their glow filled the room with love. I quickly took my seat to hide the tears of emotion welling in my eyes.

What am I actually seeing, I wondered? My eyes were certainly taking in more than usual. Why was everything glowing? Was this new expanded sight a side effect of my parking lot experience? Hopefully these overwhelming feelings of love would subside or I could look forward to being a soggy mess in the future. But this was just a glimpse of the many remarkable changes I was to undergo as I discovered the new and expanded version of me.

Foreword

What follows is an account of several years of my life after I completed the Silva Method course. This amazing workshop was designed to develop expanded awareness of the Body/Mind/Spirit connection by teaching its students to control the electrical impulses of the brain from beta waves, (waking consciousness) to the relaxed and healing, REM/sleep states of the slower alpha waves. The slower the brain emits its electrical impulses the more relaxed a person becomes. Continuing to produce the lower cycles per second (cps) a person will eventually slide in to the natural sleep state, evolving from lower alpha to theta to the unconsciousness of the low delta brain wave pattern. Repeated practice can accelerate healing and can open pathways to expanded states of consciousness.

None of my personal experiences are fantasized though they may seem so to those who are not ready to hear that we are, indeed, more than our physical bodies and five senses. We are actually more nonphysical than we are physical, expressing Being-ness throughout many dimensions of existence. We are unlimited in our human potential.

There is a possibility that my views on organized religion may offend some people. Just keep in mind the events and circumstances detailed are actually my personal experiences and beliefs pertaining to orthodoxy and in no way endeavor to challenge anyone's faith or beliefs. I use the names God, Spirit, Source, Universe, ALL That IS interchangeably without any religious connotations. This work is a reporting of my experiences, not an effort to promote any kind of philosophy, but rather an invitation to explore another perspective of time/space reality.

Initially it was difficult to live both physically and non-physically focused. Once I was determined to allow myself to explore the non-physical aspects of personal reality I began a journal for my future reference. But mere words can be miserably inadequate when dealing with events vastly removed from the usual day to day routine.

The problem, when trying to convey these intensely spiritual experiences and insights, is that they lack the emotional impact that accompanies them as they happen. If you've ever tried to share an "ah ha" moment that sends your emotions into the rafters and has your body tingling you know what I mean. Your whole being reacts to it but, in the relating of it, it falls flat on the ears of your audience. You end up saying, "I guess you had to be there."

This is an intensely personal work. There are embarrassing as well as hilarious moments. I have detailed many of my experiences as examples of mental and spiritual power that we, as intuitively aware physical beings, have at our disposal should we dare to put them to use. In my quest to understand my initial blending of non-physical and physical states of being, I opened an avenue of communication with the non-physical realms of consciousness.

Had I shared these experiences when they started to occur I would have lacked the years of research and continued personal investigation which I can now contribute. There was also the fear of ridicule I wasn't willing to risk. But as more and more people have come forward with their stories, it becomes obvious that there is so much more to physical reality than that which is experienced through our five senses.

And why am I adding yet another story on spiritual growth and para-worldly connection to the ever growing list? Because it is my belief that we are not our brother's keepers...we ARE our brothers. And we owe it to one another, in our Oneness, to share the human potential. Without reading some of the previously published accounts, I would have been at a terrible loss to understand what was happening to me, and in many instances, terrified to go on to further exploration.

To these people, I wish to give my undying gratitude for their loving help in sharing the path through their written words:

Baba Ram Das, my first guru, for <u>BE HERE NOW</u> and for introducing us to Hari Das Baba, his Yoga teacher, whose loving presence opened my daughter's heart at a Yoga temple in Coconut Grove, Florida, simply by touching her gently on the sholder.

Dr. Raymond Moody for his research on near death experiences.

Dr. John Lilly, in <u>THE CENTER OF THE CYCLONE,</u> helped me to understand that the voices I hear are my Higher Guidance.

Robert Monroe, whose wonderful facility in Faber, Virginia, The Monroe Institute, was the scene of many exciting adventures in inner and extra dimensional travel.

Esther and Jerry Hicks and Abraham for the exciting work of <u>The Law of Attraction</u>, and for their on-going work in well being for the planet.

A very special thanks to Jose Silva for his monumental contribution to education and the advancement of the spirit/mind/body connection.

And most of all to my wonderful and loving family and friends who are convinced that I am crazy and love me anyway.

If you are a neophyte spiritual explorer, I invite you to read this with an open mind. Perhaps it will become as evident to you as it is to me from reliving these experiences as I write, that our human potential is unlimited and the knowledge of that potential is invaluable as we continue to evolve towards the super Beings that we are.

Author's Note

This may help to understand why I have chosen to write as I have.

Since this written effort is all about my personal experiences you will not find many descriptive interactions between me and my family and friends within the pages unless it pertains directly to my spiritual growth. This is, after all, my story, my experiences.

Most of the dialogue is between me and my Higher Guidance as I keep a running conversation with them. It started in the beginning as I strove to understand my expanding consciousness. I then became aware of an inner communication that was very different from my normal mental ramblings. This interaction continues to this day.

For months I spoke to and referred to Higher Guidance as "The Guides, or The Guys." I had been told right off the bat that I would have no reference as to any information, visions, etc, coming from anyone or thing but myself and my Higher Guidance. The Blessed Virgin or St. Michael never spoke to me that I am aware of.

I had accepted that I received information from a source that was more intelligent and felt very different from my physical self. I was comfortable with it and, in time, I came to trust it.

Several months into my journey, during a quiet, non-meditative time, it popped into my mind that I really did not know who delivered the information. I had never even thought to ask. Deciding it was time, I took a deep breath and made my inquiry, "Who *are* you. Do you *have* a name?"

There was silence for a bit and I wondered if I would get an answer. And then, "You can call us Phil."

Let me tell you, I had a hardy laugh over that. Later in the day, still laughing at the absurdity of addressing the Guides as Phil, I thought to look up the meaning for Phil. I discovered it is a Greek root word for love. So, you will hear a lot from Phil throughout these pages.

Part One

Chapter One

Subtle Beginnings

Preparing to leave the class after the final exercise of the evening, several people asked what had happened to me during break. They agreed that I was somehow different. They could feel an energy shift when I entered the room. And they had seen my tears, of course.

We reached out to touch one another, holding hands. It seemed important to establish physical contact. We could all feel an energy moving through us and remarked on it. I could feel tears threatening to embarrass me again. But I wasn't the only one.

What we didn't realize then was that we were perceiving or experiencing one another at an energy level that was open to us in our expanded conscious mentality. We were all more open and intuitive because of the nature of the workshop.

I tried my best to relate what had happened out on the street but found words were far too inadequate to express the impact of the experience.

What happened to me was not a metaphor. It wasn't "as if" time ceased to exist. Time stood still; it was irrelevant.

And then I was swept into overdrive. Someone spoke to me in clear, calm words that I could hear with my physical ears but whom I could not see with physical sight, even though everything else in the parking lot stood out in crisp, clear resolution.

In trying to put some understanding to my experience, I was told that not everything could be understood logically. But I think what happened (and this is strictly an intellectual explanation) my physical mind relaxed and let go for a moment and I was allowed a brief glimpse of my nonphysical Being as I exist outside of space/time.

Later at home, I sat in my favorite chair frowning at a copy of the <u>United Crime Report,</u> a 200 page book of statistics compiled every year by the FBI, obsolete at the end of each year. I was supposed to be conversant with the material for the exam at 8:00 the following morning. Studying the material at this late date was out of the question. It was after midnight and I was too relaxed and sleepy. However, my compulsive self determined that I should just have a look at the book.

The final exercise of this third evening of the Silva workshop was one of the first ones designed by Jose Silva to teach elementary school students how to use intelligence to greater capacity, particularly in an academic setting. Since I was in graduate school during the Silva workshop, and had a mid-term exam the following morning, I had wanted to learn this technique really well.

Still in an expanded alpha state, I began to slowly fan through the pages. I let them stop here and there and made a casual mental note of what was on the page. After about

15 minutes, too sleepy to go on, I tossed the book aside and went to bed.

In class next morning, I was amazed to find that I knew the answers to all but one of the 100 questions on the exam even though I had not studied the material, nor had the instructor lectured on it.

The previous evening's Silva workshop had taught us that we could take tests in an alpha/expanded state of consciousness, and that would insure a more relaxed and thorough retrieval of the needed information. Also, an alpha state would allow us to probe the instructor's mind for the answer to specific questions. Many of us thought this bordered on cheating, Personally? I really did not believe it would work.

Since I had completed the exam quickly I decided to give it a try. I did this with a sense of fun and disbelief. I took a deep breath and visualized standing in front of the professor, asking him for the answer to that one question I did not know. The answer he gave me (or what popped into my mind) didn't seem right. I wasn't ready to trust what I received so I went ahead with my original answer and turned in the paper. So much for mental cheating.

The following week when we got our grades for the exam, I became the most unpopular student in the class because I broke the curve with a 99%. The next highest grade was an 82%. I had missed that one question because I had not believed the correct answer I had received mentally from probing the professor's mind! Amazing...

As an interesting aside - and I'm not recommending it, because this *is* an invasion of privacy - you can actually get information from someone with this method without them knowing it. The easiest way to get truthful answers is to catch them in their REM cycle of sleep, usually right after they have fallen asleep or just before they wake up. It helps to know their sleep patterns. And you must be in a highly receptive state yourself - deep alpha or high theta cps.

I did this only once and felt pretty awful about being so disrespectful to the person whose mind I had probed. I did, however, get correct information as verified at a later date.

If you are probing for sensitive information, be aware that that kind of information will not be given up easily, if at all, and may be given in a form of code or metaphor. This is why this type of information gathering was abandoned by the intelligence communities of several countries during the cold war period.

The Silva Method was to prove invaluable to me all the way through school. Studying at alpha level expands the mind and the memory. It is even possible to anticipate questions to be given and thus know exactly what to study. Data seems to stick in the memory and the expanded learning capacity makes it fun to study. A relaxed state relieves performance anxiety that can cloud mental acuity. We can all have this kind of genius mentality if we are encouraged to develop it.

Though the Silva Method workshop is taught on two consecutive weekends at this time, in the early days it was crammed into the students all in one unrelenting week. I believe this is why I had such an explosive psychic opening, as I really never came out of the alpha, expanded state for that whole week. We were at it from Tuesday through Friday from 7:00pm until after midnight and then most of us went home directly to sleep; more alpha and even deeper Theta wave time as is the normal sleep pattern. We had twelve hours on Saturday and another eight on Sunday. I call that total emersion.

Without explaining all the techniques of the Silva Method, suffice it to say that every member of the workshop accomplished what they came for and then some. I certainly learned to achieve relaxation. Several of us were able to program ourselves off of all tobacco products. Many shed old counter-productive behavior patterns and felt more self confident. And so much more.

Our instructor was Paul Francella, whose loving goodness and sense of humor mentored all of us sudents through that class. We graduated, a motley bunch of budding psychic healers; better coping, greater achieving, and more open and loving people. Paul was an inspiration to me. I wouldn't have had the courage to continue my metaphysical/spiritual exploration without his guidance and support.

Chapter Two

Checking In with Spirit

There is nothing like a personal experience of transformation from the ordinary to the remarkable to get your attention. I was so intrigued by what I had accomplished mentally I wanted to see what else I could do with my new found skills. Thus, I began a dedicated regiment of alpha time that consequently opened a whole new world for me. But in my case, being the extreme personality that I am, I took those Silva techniques to heart and practiced them throughout the day. Every spare 5 minutes I had I would drop into alpha. The more I practiced, the more I expanded my consciousness, and the quicker and easier it became to get there. Very soon all I had to do was take a deep breath to achieve an altered state. I became an alpha junkie!

It is probably safe to say that most people who have taken any of the numerous workshops available on the subject of mind and spirit expansion did not experience the extreme awakening that I did. As with any endeavor, you get out of it what you put in to it. But if there is anyone who has traveled these avenues and is still baffled by the results, perhaps this work will answer some of the lingering questions.

My life as a spiritual explorer, determined to answer the questions of what this whole physical experience is all about, has been the central theme of my life. I've often wondered why I was born with such a driving need to seek the answers. It became clear later on that such a clear and focused intent offers opportunity, opens doors, provides teachers.

Weeks following the workshop I had noticed some subtle and some not so subtle changes in myself. Without any real thought or effort I was evolving into a more loving and patient person. I was more generous with my time, certainly more relaxed in my approach to living in general.

And since I was totally involved in this new approach, my customary analytical outlook seemed less important. I did not need to question my every thought or action in my search for perfection. It's amazing how much time and mental energy *that* freed up. Unnecessary thoughts can hold hostage your appreciation of the moment. Mind chatter can be exhausting. With this mental freedom came the awareness of the ebb and flow of time. I noticed that if I stayed centered time could be extended. Getting uptight or anxious seemed to cut my time to a bare minimum.

Think about it. What is the mantra when one is on a tight time schedule? " Gotta hurry. Not enough time. Not enough time." Not only does it give us anxiety but it creates... not enough time.

As I was changing, my environment was morphing into a playground of ease and fun. Whatever I planned or arranged for the day seem to work out well. It became clear to me that the time I spent at alpha level centered me in the Now and provided benefits. There was no driving need to take action towards a goal. Whatever needed to get done was accomplished without striving. Being centered seemed to clear a path of resistance to any objective. Synchronicity (simultaneous occurrence) would come into play allowing all things to flow naturally and easily, even the simplest and most mundane. I began to understand that each moment provided everything I needed as long as I was present to receive. These lovely moments attended to all my needs; physical, mental, emotional and spiritual.

On the east side of Fort Lauderdale we live around the schedules of draw bridges. If you happen to catch a bridge during our winter season, traffic can back up for blocks and make you frustrated trying to get somewhere on time. In my centered state, I could leave the house, free from worry about being caught at a bridge. I had no trouble finding parking places close to where I was going, even getting meters with time still on them. Catching green lights was a breeze. The smallest of life's little necessities were made available to me. If you want to be tickled about your days, start it with an intent to honor your moments.

What I had not realized, prior to the Silva Method workshop, was that being efficient, as I had proudly defined myself, actually stressed me out. With my energy so focused in the future I was forced into anxious rushing to keep abreast of my agenda for the day. Once I arrived at any planned activity, my attention was no longer centered there but on to the next thing on the list. I had a mantra beating at the back of my brain. "Get it done, get it done, get it done,"

Being so future focused I found that most of my enjoyment of any event was often experienced in retrospect. And memory is no substitute for the real thing. We dull so much of life's enjoyment by NOT being present for ourselves.

Being present in the NOW gave me the delicious feeling of fluidity. I flowed through my moments, day to day, without friction. Most surprising was that I accomplished as much, if not more in some cases, with less effort and more joy. I was filled with a self perpetuating uplifting energy. Doing those formerly unpleasant tasks actually became fun.

Here's a game I play to determine what would be the most pleasant and efficient way to set up the following day's chores. The previous evening I make a list of those things I want to accomplish, prioritizing in order of importance. Upon morning arising, I ask myself, "What do I want to do now?" I call it "checking in." The Claudia of Yore would hit the floor at a dead run toward the thing I most wanted to get out of the way; usually the most unpleasant task.

The first time I did this exercise it was a Saturday. The kids were both off spending the weekend with grandparents and my husband was out of town on business. The item at the top of my list was to clean out and recycle a lot of good but out-grown clothes from the storage closet in the garage. A task I had been saving for just such a day without family or study interruption. I was not looking forward to it.

That morning I awoke wanting nothing more than a good cup of coffee and a cozy lay-about. But a guilty niggling at the back of my mind was pulling its old tricks and just about had me throwing back the covers, bounding out of bed, forgetting the coffee and tearing into that closet.

Old programming can be difficult to change. To avoid conflict and thereby accomplish nothing, I forced myself to lie there, get centered and ask, "What do I *really* want to do now?"

What I really wanted, of course, was to bring a cup of coffee back to bed and stare at the walls, maybe have a little alpha time. This I did, promising myself I would tackle that closet after my coffee. Wrong! After the coffee and before I left the bed, I again asked, "What do I want to do now?" The answer was to call one of my friends who was at the bottom of my to-do list. I wanted to persuade her to head up a civic committee, promising myself to do the closet after I spoke with her.

I caught her just as she was packing to leave town for several days and so was able to secure her acceptance to chair the committee. Nice timing there. I would have missed her altogether had I waited until later in the day.

Checking in began to get really fun and full of surprises. From time to time I wondered if I would ever get to the closet. Sometime after noon I asked myself if it was time to do the darn thing. "Naahhh!" So, on I went, getting tickled by what I was doing and enjoying myself enormously.

Finally around 4:00pm there was nothing left to do but the closet. I was heading in that direction when the phone rang. The call was from a volunteer friend at the Red Cross asking for donations for the survivors of a massive earthquake in Chile. The task of the closet then took on more significance than just a cleaning. It gave me a sense of emotional fulfillment. Had I taken on that closet at the beginning of the day, those clothes would have been at Goodwill and I would have missed a wonderful opportunity to participate in a worthy community effort. But most of all I would have missed a valuable opportunity to experience the fun of higher consciousness at work.

At the end of the day I had completed every item on my list and more; not in the initial order but by a higher priority that served to give me a day flowing with purpose and pleasure.

Want to know where your energy is? Be still for a minute and just feel for it. Is it firmly in your heart center or is it rushing ahead of you to the next thing on the list? If you can command a stillness, breathing naturally and easily, with your mind at rest and a feeling of peace you have arrived in your Here and Now. You know the rightness of it. When action is needed for a purpose there will be a gentle urging in the proper direction. You can trust this.

It should be noted that being present or focused in any activity you find compelling and fulfilling is an excellent example of being Here and Now. You bring your Nowness along with you, moment to moment, and this enhances your enjoyment of it. There is a Higher Intelligence available to all of us when we are fully engaged in self expressive activity and consciously aware.

Chapter Three

Spirit and the Flow

The more time I spent in expanded states the more I noticed a change in my thought patterns. I was finding that, given half a chance, Phil will not only be instructive but also very playful. I started having impressions, or thoughts that did not seem to be my own. I was often reduced to giggles by some of the new ways I chose to modify old patterns of behavior. There was a new energy at work in my life and I was fascinated by its sense of humor.

(Since I have already introduced Phil in the Author's Note you know how I came to call Higher Guidance, Phil. And I will continue to call them Phil from this point on.)

Phil has a wonderful, playful attitude about most everything. Even when I am throwing a tantrum, and I recommend this activity as a quick release of negative energy, I've never had an experience of anything but tolerant amusement or loving comfort from them. Forming a lively relationship with Phil has resulted in a lifelong love affair.

On one occasion I was trying to forestall a threatening cold. Previously, to avoid any indisposition, I would just hide out and snivel and whine in the privacy of my bed. But this was the first time I had the urge to go shopping. Let me emphasize, I am no shopper without cause. There was never time for that activity even if I had been so inclined. And I really did not feel energetic enough to satisfy the urge to shop.

I had to ask myself if I really wanted to go shopping. The answer was a resounding, "No!" In fact my energy was so low I could barely get to a meditative state.

I wondered why then this urge to shop, and with grim determination, took a deep breath and asked Phil. The answer was such a welling up of delightful expectation and renewed energy that I could hardly wait to get in the car. Without further thought I left my sick bed and drove straight to Neiman Marcus and practically ran into the couture design department. I came to a whip lashing halt in front of a lovely periwinkle blue Victor Costa design and almost burst into song. Had I the talent, I'm sure I could have composed a symphony to it.

There were so many gorgeous designs artfully displayed around each designer. I could not get enough of the feel and color of the fabrics. And truthfully, I felt a strong urge, an actual energy rush, to see and touch each designer garment. I swear, there must be one feminine consciousness within Phil. "Look! Look! See this!" urgently directed me to certain designs. Whatever was at work here was filling my senses with the beauty of the designs. I'm sure I eventually fondled every garment in that department.

After my texture and color fix was satisfied it was time to leave. On the way home I sort of came to myself and started laughing. What had I just done? It seems that I had used color and fabric and design to clear out my sinuses. I felt like a million bucks. And I had discovered a new cure for the common cold!

Several days later I returned to Neiman's and bought that Victor Costa. I wore the tail off it for years.

A funny aside; I got a call from one of my volunteer committee members telling me there would be a newspaper photo shoot and please not wear that same dress unless I wanted everyone in town thinking that was the only garment I owned.

After my fashion awakening at Neiman's I became more aware of color. Or rather, my expanded senses were better tuned to anything I chose to look at. Here again, looking and really seeing can be two different events. When you are present in the moment, everything can be experienced to the fullest. Without it, life can seem exceedingly dull.

After reading a book on the impact of color on health and environment I wanted to know my soul color for possible future healings. I knew I was strongly attracted to the warm colors, especially orange and expected that might be my color. Before sleep one night, I decided to program a dream to show me my special color. I had no idea if it would work. Dreams are often impossible to understand and notoriously unreliable.

Using intent and the alpha state, I visualized all the colors I could get my mind to conjure up and tried to tack them on a wall. It wasn't easy as the colors kept floating off my visual screen. At some point I became bored with the exercise and drifted off to sleep.

During one of my REM (dream) cycles I dreamed that I was sitting in a theatre audience expecting to watch a play. The curtain opened to a brightly lit stage. The only prop was a large coat rack, gloriously festooned with silky scarves of every imaginable color. I saw a luscious red/orange scarf that I absolutely had to have. Just as I was about to run up on the stage and grab it, an amorphous, vaguely human shaped figure floated onto the stage holding a Periwinkle Blue scarf across its formless face where its nose would be. The thing did a little shimmy and fluttered the scarf in my direction. As I reached for the compelling color of blue silk, I heard, "Use this in good health."

I woke right up, smiling and feeling full of rampant, playful energy. Unfortunately it was just past 2:00am and there was no one I dared wake to play with. No wonder I had to have that Costa design!

I'm not certain what happens to our psyches during the normal sleep cycle. But I suspect that I am often cavorting in the nonphysical realms. I have on many occasions awakened with impressions, and actual words of instructions. One of my favorite one liners from the dreamscape was handed down as if gospel, strongly and emphatically uttered. "The ideal citizen of the Universe is a man [sic] who sees a job needs doing, and does it." Where had I been to have brought that back with me?

Another such instance occurred when I was anticipating taking an important written career test that had a choice of dates. I was actually abruptly awakened by what felt like a slap to my face and someone shouted, "For God's sake take the test before April 6th". I did, of course, but to this day I have no idea why that date was important.

Becoming consciously aware that I was more than my physical body and my five senses was a startling revelation since I had been so caught up in seeking outward validation of my personal worth. Understanding that I was not my achievements, I began to see cracks in the defenses I had constructed to hide feelings of inadequacies. It became apparent that rushing around to excel at everything I undertook was not only exhausting but so unnecessary.

Awakening to the Spirit within made me want to be a better, more authentic person.I really had no clue as to who or what I was. Without my grand scheme to label myself Super Mom and Wife, or Psychologist, who was I? Because my Inner Guidance was so committed to "growing me up," I finally came to accept that no amount of activity, accomplishment or effort would ever be enough to make me feel worthy or valuable if I had no connection to the God/ Spirit within. That in itself is a grand reason for being.

This was brought home to me one night as I contemplated where I was going with this program of spiritual expansion. I had asked if it was even necessary that I know. I must have slipped into an expanded state, for vividly on my mental screen and independent of my imagination, I had a vision of myself in an operating theatre, bright lights focused on me as I lay naked on a table covered by a large white sheet. Masked surgeons surrounded the table and began by stripping the sheet from my body with a flourish, tossing it aside.They then began removing "things" from my skin, probing into the muscles, organs, tossing bits and pieces over their shoulders until I lay bare to my bones. I actually saw myself as a skeleton stretched out on that table.

I was embarrassed and appalled at what I saw removed from my body. Each layer peeled away an emotional block; fears, limitations, negative beliefs, judgments. The insights were astounding as I grasped just how little I had loved and accepted myself; just how much I had chased after public acknowledgment and romanced my family and friends for my fix of self endorsement.

As I lay there, bare to the bones, absorbing these insights, the operation began in reverse. The doctors commenced putting me back together, fleshing my skeleton; filling my body with love blindingly pure and illuminated with the knowledge of my personal Divinity. I felt every molecule, every cell vibrate and sing with the light of Source.

I understood that any remnant of self loathing and unworthiness would be a denial of my Divine connection. Refusing that gift of light and love would have meant spiritual death. Ask anyone who has refused God's love and they will affirm that. Every soul on Earth, every tiny cell, every molecule within the Multiverse is a spark of the Divine Creator. This is what we all Are and that is *ALL* we need to know about our worth. We do not have to deserve it or work for it, and we certainly do not have to suffer for it. It is inherent by virtue of our Divine connection to our Creator.

Chapter Four

Spirit and Nature

I cannot remember a time when I wasn't interested in all forms of religions, both ancient and modern, Eastern and Western. As a child I did not have the concept of spirit as being different from religion. I do have very early memories of voices I dialogued with. My Guardian Angels, I was told. They kept me company at night as I was falling asleep.

My youthful need to acknowledge my spiritual nature sought to express itself through the orthodoxy of Catholicism. I embraced the faith thoroughly and completely, vowing to lead an exemplary life. If I had had the knowledge and experience of maturity, I would have realized that I am a pan-Theist at heart. I feel God or Spirit in everything. That is why most metaphysicians call God, ALL THAT IS. Phil is fond of reminding me. «Since ALL THAT IS is actually all that is, there is nothing that is not sacred.»

Even as a child I felt Spirit present in the natural world. Nature was a constant source of delightful adventure. Nothing could beat hiding out in my favorite tree, where my carved initials announced that this was my special place. Many of my burning questions concerning my young life were discussed with that tree as well as early morning conversations with my horse. In fact even now I get some of my best insights from the flora and fauna in my environment. Try chatting up a tree you find attractive. Its wisdom will amaze you.

But somewhere between the magic of childhood and the responsibilities and practicalities of adulthood I lost personal contact with Nature, to the point of being the family joke when it came to anything potted and green. No one gave me a house plant unless they wanted a dried arrangement within two weeks. Some plants just took one look at me and keeled over instantly.

A couple of years prior to the Silva experience my mother-in-law gave me her collection of beloved orchids when she sold the family home and moved to a condo on the beach. Those orchids had been her hobby and passion for years and she was rightly proud of them. She helped me hang those beauties in our screened patio, finding just the right place for their maximum flowering potential. We had many talks about how to care for them. She was leaving me with her babies to nurture and love. This responsibility she laid on my sholders caused me many sleepless nights. I prayed for those things to thrive.

Anyone who has raised orchids knows that they practically thrive on neglect in the subtropics. Ah, the perfect plant for me it would seem. Within a few months my patio looked like a prime example of the scorched earth policy; shriveled and brown stalks hanging all over the walls. When it became obvious that those pathetic twigs would never thrive nor bloom I began making excuses for my mother in law to avoid the patio area. That poor woman's face when she finally did get past me to the patio…It wasn't pretty.

The growing of healthy greenery was an exercise in futility as far as I was concerned until the remarkable shift in my energy through daily alpha sessions.

During one quick trip to the supermarket wheeling a grocery cart past a stand of very healthy, feathery ferns, I heard, "Hey there!" I stopped, glancing around to see who had called me but no one was close by. Thinking I was mistaken, I started back up the aisle. But then I felt a tug of energy calling my attention back to the plants. I was captivated by their fresh and vibrant green. As I stood contemplating their beauty, I heard again, "Hey there!"

Feeling a bit silly I looked surreptitiously over each shoulder to make sure I was alone and then put my face right down into the ferns and whispered, "What? Did you call me?" Silence… apparently the ferns were not in the mood for further conversation. But I grabbed a particularily vibrant fern anyway, hoping I wasn't condemning the poor little plant to certain death.

When I pulled the fern out of the sack later, I wandered around the house, chatting to my new green friend, looking for a place to put the thing. I finally settled on the library table in the foyer. I felt a strong sense of pleasure as we neared the table.

"This must be your place," I said.

Fern replied, "Here!" Fern wasn't a great communicator but she got her point across. She had wanted out of the noise and garish lights of the supermarket and had found in me someone who could accommodate her.

Every time I walked pass Fern there after, I spoke to her. Fern was special, my first success, and the first of many potted bits of greenery to find residence on the library table in the foyer and throughout the house.

Soon after that small success, I graduated from the floral department in the supermarket to cruising the lawn and garden shops about town. Where I had avoided these places in the past, I now spent some part of my free time visiting them. I rarely come home empty handed. Plants, potting soil, planting paraphernalia, books, even earth worms were also purchases. If you love gardening, you'll agree there is nothing like a greenhouse full of lush and colorful plants to make you feel happy and excited about your day.

I was becoming quite conversant in plant speak. I would stroll through the greenhouses, lightly trailing a hand through the greenery, extending an open invitation to anything that wanted to come home with me. The house began to look like a nursery itself. At one point my husband asked if I had noticed that the humidity level was nearing jungle saturation in the foyer. He swore that he would soon need a machete to find the front door.

I want to emphasize that I was not doing anything different in the way of caring for plants. I had always enjoyed and admired the beauty of potted greenery and cared for them in the prescribed ways. I came to understand that my erstwhile stressed and anxious energy had been actually toxic to growing plants. My contracted, uptight energy was too strong for the gentle vibrations of the greenery to neutralize. A steady diet of unpleasant energy will eventually suppress growth. But there was something now patently different in my personal energy that was encouragement for plants to thrive. Anything I brought into the house flourished, no matter what shape it arrived in. There was a loving communication between the plants and me. We created joy within our environment. They taught me that happy, loving energy is the most healing, thriving force on earth.

After the success of the indoor plants, vegetable gardening began to interest me. Everyone warned me that I would encounter difficulties green farming in South Florida a block from the beach. I did a little research on soil and I can recommend reading Peter Tompkins and Christopher Bird's <u>SECRETS OF THE SOIL.</u> Laying a good bed or foundation for growth is essential to a thriving garden. (a metaphor for life wouldn't you agree?) The children and I had a great time getting barefoot and stomping Milgrow (Milwaukee organic fertilizer) and clean dirt into the planned bed. We bought a container of earthworms and set them free in the garden soil. Needless to say the garden flourished. And consequently, so did my cooking.

Another notable change was the glaring fact that I was beginning to enjoy homemaking…all facets of it. In the past, I had thought that being a homemaker and mother was not enough to offer the world. I must do something else equally important. Thus, when the children reached school age I went back to school for an advanced degree. I was heavily invested in succeeding as a student when the Silva Method became a necessity. Striving to excel at everything can actually kill you, so my doctor said.

With the feminist movement in full swing women felt the pressure to succeed beyond normal bounds. We were tired of being "the little woman." We wanted equal voice. I was out to prove my personal excellence.

After the Silva course I eased up to the point of "no sweat." I was no longer a driven woman. I was having so much fun being at home that my ambitions to save the world were drifting away on the puff and whisper of a beguiling slip of green. Besides, I was told quite emphatically that the world did not need saving. One night washing dishes, my mind blissfully quiet, Mother Earth spoke "I have endured and will continue to endure. Humanity must look to itself." Well, I was thankfully relieved of that responsibility!

That meant that I was free to play and not feel guilty. I did not have to accomplish great things every day. I could sing to my plants and chant around the house all day if I wanted to, or take my children and their friends to the park or beach to just goof off in silly, imaginative play. The interesting thing was that in so doing, when time came to head out for class or cook dinner, or drive the children to activities, the happy urgings to be front and center with that was never a cause for resistance. Being There and doing the job was as much fun as play. It actually became part of life's entertainment.

Life's entertainment...that recalls to mind a discussion I had with a classmate regarding how my life was changing because of the Silva Method. Most of my friends and colleagues were familiar with my intense approach to "doing the job"...my words to describe everyday living. When it became apparent that I was easing up and smiling more, my friends were interested to know why. My answer was that I had formally perceived "the job" as work, whereas now I perceived it as play or entertainment. An amazing difference.

Thankfully I had only one term after my current one to graduation and residency. I was maintaining a 3.5 GPA; doing the housework and gardening; spending more quality time with my family. Reflecting on that time it was amazing to me how active I was and that I never felt stressed; stretched on occasion, but not stressed. I was up before six most mornings and rarely in bed before one or two. I give full credit to those snatches of restful alpha time I did throughout the day. I was relaxed and at peace with myself and my life.

Chapter Five

Spirit and Religion

As I continued to allow my consciousness to expand, I began to experience spontaneous visions. That is to say, visions not orchestrated by me through a Silva technique or creative visualization. They were startling at first. Scary. I made frantic phone calls to Paul Francella to tell him I thought I might be going crazy, that I was seeing things. To do him credit he never laughed. He assured me that I was opening up my psychic channels and not to fight it. He also wanted to emphasize that I could decide to discontinue the psychic expansion at any time. I only had to make clear intent and the channel would close. He reminded me that we are free to make choices at every juncture of our lives. Hearing that, I felt comforted and assured that I could continue with my spiritual exploration without fear of insanity. I say this half in jest, but I wonder how many people are diagnosed as mentally unstable because they had no foundation in psychic research or frame of reference for an expanding consciousness.

My irreverent sense of humor has always been a constant source of amusement. Being more consciously expanded my thoughts became very entertaining (not that they weren't usually) and I often found the absurdities of life cause for hilarity. It seemed that I just couldn't take life so seriously any more. In my "saner" moments I wondered if that in itself wasn't cause for alarm. But let me make this perfectly clear, a well developed sense of humor will save your psychological hiney when everything else fails. The negative or darker emotions cannot stand up to humor.

All winter and spring terms I had been devouring books on religions and philosophies of the world. I just couldn't take in enough information to suit my need to differentiate between spirit and religion. I was particularly drawn to the Eastern philosophies, probably because they were more intellectual than emotional. Eastern thought and discipline seemed broader in scope and very mentally satisfying.

But my spiritual exploration was opening up avenues of emotion that I could not deny; emotions that clamored for expression. I was full to overflowing with joy. I needed to give thanks for the blessings of my new life.

These new and expanded feelings of love and happiness felt Holy, intensely personal and spiritual, whereas before, my outlook on spirit and consciousness had been more mental or intellectual. It was now becoming obvious that I had awakened some powerfully positive emotions. I didn't know what to do with them. But I knew they were leading me somewhere.

Having given up on orthodox Christianity several years previously, I considered myself a recovering Catholic. I rejected traditional Christian teachings as restrictive and often senseless. As youngsters in Catholic school we were fed catechism every day. We were taught to glorify suffering as an accepted way of life that would get us to Heaven. And getting to heaven was a recommended goal of life. We were told to believe the doctrines or face the loss of heaven and the fires of hell. You can bet that screwed up a few tender little minds!

So, eventually coming to believe the Catholic/Christian doctrine to be the all time great thief of psychological and spiritual freedom, I refused to even consider anything Christian. How my natural spiritual propensity was going to find an acceptable emotional expression became the burning question.

At some point in my voracious reading I found a sentence underlined and in caps in one of the books. It read: NOW IS THE TIME FOR THE STUDENT TO STOP READING AND FIND A SPIRITUAL ADVISOR. Well! It couldn't fail to catch my attention since there was no logical reason for those words to be all in caps and underlined. They fairly jumped off the page at me. I closed the book and contemplated how I would accommodate this suggestion. Sitting at some guru's feet had a certain appeal. I had no doubt that the underlined statement held great importance for me.

It is interesting to note that when I went back to that book looking for the underlined and uppercased sentence I could not fine it anywhere in the pages! Had it actually been there or was that what my nonphysical mind deemed important and how my physical eyes perceived it?

My life was so full of magical direction at this point that I was comfortable with the knowledge that everything in my physical reality was communicating with me, teaching me, helping me expand my consciousness. Years later, I know this can be true for each and every soul enjoying this space/time reality. All we need to do is become aware of it and learn to trust the information, with harm to none.

The solution to finding a spiritual advisor was swift in coming. The Silva Method generously opens its classes to its graduates for unlimited sessions, at no additional cost, for recharging or just to better condition a particular technique. I had dropped in on the classes from time to time to see friends and let Paul Francella know how I was progressing. I don't think he had many, if any, students who wanted to explore the inner or expanded realms as far as I did. He was as intrigued by what I was doing as I was.

I decided to attend the last two days of a workshop to see if the Laboratory Technique would benefit my search for a spiritual advisor. As I explained this to Paul he pressed home the fact that I was fully capable of doing that on my own, that I did not need the workshop. It was just a tool to help focus the mind. But I wanted the extra help and energy of the others present. Multiple positive energies, focused to a collective point can act as a power boost. It can also provide a comfort zone.

This was one of the few times I had asked anything in particular of the techniques, other than answers to my incessant questions. Previously I had just played with them, perfecting them, but had no agenda. I was unsure as to what to expect from wanting a certain result. Hopefully this exercise would provide an answer to my search for a spiritual advisor.

The laboratory exercise involves going to alpha level and building an imaginary place in which to work, a safe haven, where one goes to relax, solve problems, and create at an expanded level of consciousness. A "happy place", as some refer to that special mental imagery. After the laboratory has been mentally designed, we then visualize elevator doors that slide open to introduce us to our guides. The guides can be anyone or anything our imagination conjures up to help us in our mental activities; an imaginative aid for mind expansion and creative visualization. It is excellent guided imagery that keeps the mind chatter down to a minimum and makes for an easier slide into an expanded state.

In the initial workshop of this exercise my guides presented themselves to me. I did not consciously create them. I was somewhat surprised to see who did appear. Since I had been studying so much Eastern philosophy, I half expected to see Buddhist monks or the Dahli Lama when the elevator doors opened.

My guides were Native Americans, a young male named Running Fox and his mother. Running Fox did all the communicating. His mother just hung around looking solemn; occasionally nodding her head to agree with her son. Both were associated with love and they did help me with my psychic development because that is how the Silva Method taught us to interact with our guides. I could ask them questions and they would supply answers. Interesting, yes? There are many ways to obtain information from our Higher Intelligence: prayer, meditation, tarot cards, I Ching, etc. The answers are there for us. We just have to find a way to ask the questions and hear the answers that are comfortable for us.

That evening I went into the laboratory exercise with great expectations. I felt sure that the guides would introduce me to my guru. As it turned out crafty Phil had other things in store for me.

At the proper time the elevator doors slid open and there stood Running Fox and Mother with what looked like a large laundry bag. There was obviously something inside. I could see the sides of the bag were bulging and heaving as if something was struggling to get out. Running Fox shrugged, looking apologetic. Mother was smirking and I was frankly baffled and disappointed.

I suppose that Running Fox and Mom felt they were turning me over to other guidance, even though I could not see who or what was in that bag. They never showed up in my laboratory again.

After the session Paul asked me what results I'd had. He laughed when I told him what happened and said, "That ought to tell you something. I have a feeling you're not going to get what you want. Perhaps you're not ready for the answer."

Everyone was asleep when I got home, so I flopped into my favorite chair, took a deep breath and immediately slid into alpha. But instead of being inside, I found myself standing outside of my laboratory, looking at the door. *Interesting,* I thought, since I had not created a door. I was always inside my lab. *These sessions are beginning to take on a life of their own,* I mused.

The door to the laboratory was promptly opened by Mrs. Bluejeans. who was, in real life, my part time house keeper from Jamaica. We called her Mrs. Bluejeans because her lovely, lilting Jamaican accent made it difficult at first to understand the actual pronunciation of her name.

Mrs. Bluejeans was a 20 something, beautiful lady on a mission. She had come to this country to get her nursing degree and help finance the immigration of her family to a better life here in the US. She helped me to care for my house and children a couple of days a week and I helped her get a better idea of American culture. We had many lively and enjoyable conversations. Soon after her arrival in Florida she told me she had "found the Lord," and was often given to expressions of praise that were both sweet and vigorous.

Surprised to see her, I exclaimed, "Mrs. Bluejeans! What are you doing in my laboratory?"

Didn't I say these sessions were beginning to have a life of their own? I also want to emphasize that these visions were as clear to me as virtual reality, precise and in color. I was actually present within them. Someone could make a good argument for an alternate reality.

She replied with a big smile on her sweet face. "I'm here to soften the way for the one who is to be your spiritual advisor." With that, she made a flourishing sweep with her arm and revealed the person standing behind her.

When I saw who was standing there, grinning like a fool with his hand outstretched, I just dropped my chin to my chest and whined, "Oh no, this is not acceptable."

The person before me, one I had certainly NOT consciously chosen was Dr. James, a young PhD. in the department who taught psych courses with a Christian philosophy. How he managed to get his course program approved by the department chair, none of us could even imagine. The man was a known Jesus freak. I had overheard the other instructors moaning about the complaints from the students concerning Dr. James. But the department head liked him. And though he considered the man naïve and unprepared for the current generation, he approved the way Dr. James taught his classes.

Interesting to note, I later realized that I had scheduled a class without knowing he was teaching it.

"Yep, you've got me, Babe." Staring at him in disbelief, questions flitted across my mind. *Why is he talking like that? That is not his normal speech pattern. Who does he think he is, Sonny Bono?*

Though I did not know him, I had seen Dr. James in the halls at school. The man was not hip in real life. The man could have been plucked right out of the post war generation of the 50's, even though he was probably in his mid to late 20's. He wore out-dated clothes and strange shoes; his hair was military short. Obviously his appearance did not matter to him. He was not a bad looking man, rather attractive actually; just so 50s vintage.

I would never have deliberately envisioned this scenario. This person was so far removed from anyone I would even have given the space of a thought. He was a Christian, for Christ's sake! And here he was in my personal laboratory, smiling as if he had every right to be there, and announcing that *he* was to be my spiritual advisor.

I snapped out of alpha level so fast it gave me a headache. I crawled into bed feeling a confusion and dismay I did not want to deal with. And for the week there after, I stewed, agonized, and generally ranted to Phil to explain this farce!

Phil just kept their own counsel but I could sense their amusement. "This is NOT funny!," I could be heard addressing the ceiling. (For some reason I still think of heaven or nonphysical reality as vaguely up or out there.) On more than one occasion I saw my children looking up at the ceiling and asking, "What's wrong with the ceiling, Mom?"

In the end it came down to whether or not I was serious about continuing my spiritual pursuits. The operative word here was spiritual not religious. I could only assume that anything Dr. James had to teach me had to be of a Christian religious nature. And I was absolutely certain I did not want to entertain any aspect of that. I envisioned all sorts of Bible thumping and rantings of chapter and verse. At the very least I was aware of how some of the protestant religions viewed psychic research. The devil's handy work! God only knows where I got all those prejudices. Too many old movies, I guess, not to mention that I was brought up in the Southern Bible Belt and Catholic girl's boarding schools.

So, deciding to trust the whole process, I made an appointment with Dr. James for the following week. I was a nervous wreck. This was the first time I would actually share my path and experiences with anyone other than my Silva instructor. It was such an internal process my husband wasn't even aware of my spiritual flights. However, I had faith in the Universal Law that says any person who presents him/herself with sincerity and humility to any spiritual advisor would find acceptance.

With that in mind, I sat staring into the relaxed and pleasant face of the man who, at some level of consciousness, I had chosen to help me along my spiritual path.

I introduced myself. He nodded a greeting. There was no small talk. He asked me to tell him why I had sought an appointment.

As I began to speak, my voice was too high and not altogether steady from the nervous constriction of my throat. I tried to listen to myself as I would imagine Dr. James must be hearing my story.(That made me feel a little schizophrenic) I told my story fast and without any punctuation, thoroughly convinced that the instant I drew a breath he would seize that moment to throw me out of his office.

I spoke of my psychic/spiritual awakening during the Silva workshop, the changes in my personal ambitions, my relaxed states of mind, my energy shifts that had opened communication between me and the natural world and that I was experiencing visions and hearing voices.

I continued, my voice squeezed in my throat after a good 15 minutes of explanation, wanting to just get it over with…"I am experiencing visions and now this new driving desire to know God and find an acceptable expression for my spiritual longings and I even bought this book with the underlined statement to seek a spiritual advisor though it should probably be a Buddhist monk or an eastern guru of some sort instead of a Christian because I didn't really believe in the Christian myth anymore and what you, Dr. James, can do to help me I really can't say but here I am…" Whew! I spewed it all out in one breath and almost passed out from lack of oxygen. Instead I got the hiccups.

There I sat on the edge of my chair, which by this time had cut off the circulation in my thighs, hiccupping and waiting for the axe to fall. All through my recitation the man never moved a muscle nor did his eyes leave my face. He continued to stare at me in his rather vague way and I began to think that maybe he had fallen asleep with this eyes open. As I made a slight move to rise from my awkward seating position, he leaned back in his chair and spoke to me in the most normal tone of voice.

"Claudia, the Lord told me to be expecting a spiritual student any day now. I didn't know who it would be but I'm ready for you." I'm sure my eyebrows left my forehead at this point. The Lord was speaking to him? He was ready? OMG!

He reached for a stack of audio tapes (20 hours worth!) there on his desk and a large notebook filled with writing, clippings and articles. He handed these to me and told me to get started reading and listening and that we would spend two to three hours a week discussing what I was learning. My mouth fell open. I know, because that awful sound I heard could only have been caused by my hiccupping with an open mouth.

He said, as I lurched from my chair, "I'm pleased you are interested. Praise the Lord!"

I left in a state of shock. Praise the Lord? PRAISE THE LORD? He actually said that. Nobody, I determined through clenched teeth would ever make me praise the lord in a Christian fashion. I felt so betrayed by myself that I started to cry. What had I let myself in for?

If you're wondering why I continued with my spiritual quest if what I encountered was so distasteful, the answer is simply that I had come to trust the flow of Spiritual energy that moved me along the path. I believed in what I was doing even though I didn't know where it would lead. There was a strong inner urging. What's more, I couldn't seem to stop doing it.

Dr. John Lilly wrote in <u>CENTER OF THE CYCLONE</u>:

> The ruthless nature of Cosmic love (baranka) has been shown to us…Cosmic love loves and teaches you whether you like it or not; it has an inevitability a fullness of taking over, a fateful joyous quality that spreads and brings others to you teaching through you. (1972, p. 229)

I would just ask you to reread those words and take in the import of them. Even now those words are still powerful and relevant. Spirit/God LOVES us whether we like it or not, and brings joy and purpose to our lives. I find that both amazing and comforting.

In spite of how I felt initially about the advisor, I gave myself up to reading and studying the material that Dr. James had given me. It made me tremendously uncomfortable. I wasn't interested in Christianity, though the man Jesus was intriguing. (They are not necessarily mutually inclusive you know)

I had left the Catholic Church because I could no longer buy the senseless dogma. I found nothing insirational in a religion that was formalized by a group of men back in the 4th century and had not grown with the times. (Although the present pontiff Francis, is doing an excellent job of moving the Catholic Church into the 21 Century, through his intelligence and forward thinking). It was an outmoded religion of men who had decreed three hundred years *after* his death that Jesus was divine and the only son of God; a religion that was full of outdated ritual, borrowed from many of the old pagan cults. It told us how to think, what to eat and when to eat it, left no room for questions and doubt. It was a convenient and political religion of men for power.

It was my experience that the Christian tenets were not the loving, gentle wisdom of Jesus. One need only to examine history to realize that. And look at what the early conventions did to one of Jesus' favorite disciples, Mary Magdalene. Because she was a woman, they decided she must have been a camp following prostitute and condemned her forever in holy scripture. They then decided no one got to heaven except through the priests and precepts of the church.

I felt God's presence more in a walk along the beach, skiing down a mountain of fresh powder, or just watching a newborn foal gain its legs. I have a delightful Danish friend, Inger Marie, who shared an old Danish saying that has come to be one of my favorite quotes. "It is far better to be out fishing, thinking about God, than to be in church thinking about fishing." Do you love it?

At the time I was studying with my advisor it was the late 70's. The drug culture that had blossomed in the 60's was in full swing and the drop out rate was monumental. Many of those addictive personalities who had survived the drug scene desperately needed some hard structure in their lives. Many were scooped up by cults only to became religion junkies.

In Fort Lauderdale the beach area was full of them, handing out pamphlets and preaching salvation. It was a very distressing thing to witness. Perhaps some part of my discomfort came from the feeling that my irreverent sense of humor would have me down at the beach, handing out literature and praising the Lord with those poor souls. To me, it seemed like they had just traded one dependency for another, both of which can do great psychological damage to a dependent personality. And I really, *really* disliked any public emotional rantings of religious fervor.

My sessions with Dr. James started out intellectually, with comparisons between Eastern and Western thought and religion. I came to appreciate the man's intelligence and scope of knowledge. He knew a great deal about Eastern philosophy. And I soon discovered he wasn't a Jesus freak but simply and completely loved Jesus Christ and His teachings. Dr. Jame's faith was a beautiful energy that surrounded him and made him a happy man. The man knew what worked for him.

Dr. James taught me to look at all orthodox religions as discipline, a good place to start a path to a spiritual/religious understanding of ourselves. If a certain path gets you where you want to go, continue on. It was the first time since I'd rejected my Catholic education that I even entertained the idea that all paths that lead to Spirit/God have validity.

Phil told me that faith has nothing to do with the man made edicts of any religion. Orthodoxy, as expressed in church, becomes just a place to show up on Sundays. And, depending upon who is standing at the pulpit, can be informative and uplifting. Faith is a knowing and trusting, an absolute conviction of something greater than ourselves. Spirit/God endorses all forms of acknowledgement. Because, in that acknowledgment, we are recognizing our Divine connection.

Another remarkable thing about Dr. James was his humility. I must have been absolutely insufferable in my attitude that he couldn't teach me anything important. My mind had slammed shut and no Christian crowbar was going to pry it open. I was startled to find that my mind was just as closed as I had supposed all believing Christian minds were. But little by little Dr. James was winning my respect. He never rebuked me for my arrogant attitude. He was loving and patient and confident that I would come to see the Light.

Concurrent with my studies with Dr. James I was still developing my psychic abilities. By that I mean I was still practicing altering my state of consciousness, "going to level." Using the alpha state, I was not leading myself in any particular direction; no agenda other than exploration; opening to the possibilities. And there are many. I saw visions and heard voices, communicated with all manner of creatures, both plant and animal through an ever widening telepathic and empathetic channel.

Empathy is a natural fallout of altered states. Expanded states bring us to a oneness with our physical and non-physical reality. This is where inter-dimensional communication takes place. I could experience the thoughts and feelings of others. I was not altogether comfortable with this turn of events but I was learning to handle it. Empathy is an excellent tool for Marriage and Family counseling as I would find out during my residency.

However, I loved the communication with plants and animals. They love the attention and will go on and on if you let them. Their wisdom will amaze and delight you.

A big White Fir told me once as I stood before it, bemoaning the loss of almost half of its branches after transplanting, "Do not fear for us. We are in the process of defoliating that part of us that no longer benefits our physical whole. And that which is shed is joyfully released to reunite with the non-physical expression of our greater aspect. We will survive and thrive by releasing that which no longer serves to make room for that which does." Nature, through its wisdom, has so much to teach us.

While none of these things are the average daily fare for most folks, they were gradually becoming acceptable to me. Occasionally I would question my sanity, do a reality check. But after the initial surprise of the expanded senses, I began to feel quite easy with them. There were many times when I wondered where the ceiling was. Just how far could I go with these expanded states? I was not long in finding the answer.

During this time there seemed to be an accelerated sense of a presence, a loving "Other." I asked Phil if I could see this presence and when I opened my eyes at the close of the meditation I saw a wheel-like swirl of white energy almost as high as the ceiling roll through the living room. When I asked what it was, I was told. "That is God dancing in your living room." I came to understand that God loves an opportunity to show off like that. Apparently, the more we seek the Light the more we see the Light.

Years later, while attending an Earthwright's blessing of a friend's farm in upstate New York, several of us saw a similar swirl of luminous energy roll through the middle of the circle of those gathered. There was God, dancing Its blessing on the farm. Spirit is ever with us.

In opening to the Light, I was coming to appreciate the Christian teachings more and more. But instead of feeling good and easy about this I found that it was causing me emotional conflict. My compulsive personality wanted everything in tidy packages, properly labeled. The package marked "Christianity" had been put aside as obsolete and restrictive. I never wanted to open that package again. I had spent years deprogramming my Catholic brainwashing. I no longer had bad dreams about leaving the church and facing hell under the horizon. It still makes me angry to think that any institution could hold minds hostage through fear of damnation for daring to question man made doctrine.

Doing dishes one evening I had a strong vision of a vast, unending landscape with one tiny person trying to build a fence around its perimeter. Truly an impossible task. The message was loud and clear; "There is no way to build a fence around God. God is greater than any religion and yet belongs to all of them."

The more I was intellectually willing to expand my appreciation of the Christian ethic the more I kept running into an emotional conflict. This presented a snag in my otherwise harmonious existence. The more I tried to resolve the problem the more disturbed I became. I knew the time was fast approaching when I would have to deal with this conflict yet again but I was not looking forward to it.

Chapter Six

Spirit and Conflict

Since I had been seeking expanded self expression, I had given my mental/emotional self permission to clear the course for further spiritual exploration without really understanding the zeal with which my psyche and Phil were willing to undertake the program. I had said, "…whatever it takes," and had then gone about my days totally unprepared for the consequences of that simple statement. Without much thought, I just kept saying "yes!" to the opportunities I attracted to further grow spiritually.

The psyche is a repository of all things mental and emotional from the moment of conception and even beyond. It can flood the brain with endorphins for our happy memories or release adrenalin and fear surrounding negative belief systems in truly creative ways.

Suppressed fear will find a way to surface. It nudges against its mental and emotional boundaries until it finally exposes itself. Denial only makes fear stronger until, at last, it must be acknowledged. Fear will often cleverly disguise itself as other negative emotions such as anger, anxiety, aggressiveness and can generally create havoc in our lives. Suppressed fear can make us sick mentally, emotionally and physically.

My fearful resistance around the conflict of the Christian religion versus my spiritual pursuits took the path of bizarre thoughts. I developed anxiety about walking through my living room. And in the dark, forget about it! I found it both weird and amusing. Sadly, the fear was keeping me from my favorite meditation chair. My sense of humor was failing me at this point, even though I knew rationally that there was nothing scary in living room. There was just a contracted, negative feeling that swamped me as I approached the living room.

Something bad is in that room, floated through my mind.

One night as I was falling asleep I felt the need to go to the bathroom. When I threw back the cover to get out of bed I was filled with a fleeting, but horrifying, thought that, as I passed my sewing area, I would grab the scissors and stab every member of my family and the dog to death, a maniacal rampage. I was instantly paralyzed with fear. My mind was racing in all directions, my heart was pounding, and I broke out in a sweat. Panic! Would I, could I really do such a horrifying thing? Here my liberating sense of humor kicked in and I asked, *"What about all the little fish in the pond? Do they get it too?"*

I lay huddled under the covers, pressed up against my husband's back trying to pull myself together. Where did those dark thoughts come from? I suspected that this was my psyche banging on the door for attention. It had caught me at an opportune time with my mental defenses relaxed to make a point. Its subtle clues had gone unattended.

Apparently is was time to bring out the big guns and scare the daylights out of myself.

Being a student of psychology was a blessing in this instance and saved me with cold reason. No power on earth would have had me harm my family, no matter how conflicted I was emotionally. But there is a repository of darkness in all of us. It lies dormant within the primitive part of our brains that helped us survive as we developed into the human beings we are today. Old fears from mass consciousness, cultural beliefs, even scary movies when we were children can hide out in unconscious memory and can surface during times of psychological crisis. And of course, we humans dearly love to scare ourselves, just to get our juices flowing.

Taking a good hard look at the situation made it abundantly clear. In order to open the way for further spiritual advancement my emotional conflict around religion had to be addressed. It was time to get over it.

Getting to the bottom of emotional dissonance is much like solving a murder mystery. "Who or what murdered my peace of mind?" It requires asking pertinent questions, brutal honesty, and deciphering a trail of clues.

At the core of my mystery, clothed in bizarre fears, were my feelings of losing control of my spiritual freedom. But you don't solve deep seated, suppressed fears at an intellectual level. You bring them to consciousness so you can deal with them at an emotional level. Also, taking the fears to an absurdly exaggerated level and having a good laugh over them will help face the issues.

There are those that want to make the ego the bad guy. But the ego (the little self) has the job of keeping us physically focused; necessary for time/space reality. Mine had been holding sway for the greater portion of my adult life. My super ego (the expanded or Multidimensional Self), whose job it is to maintain a balance between body, mind and spirit, was clamoring for a level playing field. I had to get off the emotional teeter-totter and find that harmonious resonance again. I did not know how I was going to accomplish this. I decided to question Phil.

Spirit has a way of insinuating change within us. It may start in small niggling ways and if not given the proper attention will began, as it did with me, to cause problems. Though it isn't really the change that causes the actual problem, it is the resistance to change that is the real culprit, as I was soon to discover.

I quickly deduced that my irrational fear of the living room stemmed from my meditating there every day. My crafty ego was saying, in essence, that by scaring me out of the living room I would no longer meditate. Fear of harming my loved ones would keep me immobilized and stuck in the status quo. I would then remain a slave to past conditioning and old programs and remain thoroughly focused in the physical. That would eliminate spiritual growth. Endeavoring to neutralize the ego, I would have to let go of a lifetime of conditioning, defense mechanisms, and self image. No small feat that! Was I up to that challenge?

I chose to settle the issue by arising before dawn and, in the dark, begin a meditation in a corner of the livingroom with most of the room to my back. This room was a rectangle 33 foot long, 16 feet wide and with high ceilings cantilevered by heavy wooden beams. I felt like I was in a large cave. All my childish fears of the dark came creeping up my back, chilling my mind. I had difficulty controlling my active imagination and started to hyperventilate. I got light headed and thought I might faint.

I launched into a fervent prayer for help. I was rescued by the loving presence of Phil offering me a prayer of Light to encircle myself. The prayer blessed me with peace and a feeling of safety. So, you see, help is there for us if we but ask. And the living room and my favorite chair were once again mine. Fear cannot stand up to Light.

We do not realize that when we begin to expand consciousness that there is a metaphorical door that we must open to the nonphysical realms. It opens for us in fleeting moments but slams shut quickly unless we practice the vibrational resonsance to keep it open. And standing before that door with blazing swords is a magnificent dragon. All of our deep seated fears from childhood, from mass consciousness, from curtural myths, and possibly from pass lives, come to the fore. It is only through love that we are able to slay the dragon and enter. Jesus called it the Kingdom of Heaven. And we do not have to die to attain it. But I was not there yet.

As the sessions with my advisor progressed, I had begun to experience spontaneous and persistent visions of a large hand containing tiny round objects, like BBs. Every now and then the BBs would slip between the fingers and start to spill. I understood that this was another metaphor. My psyche was telling me in vision speak that it was in fear of losing control again. I managed to restrain the vision somewhat but found it disturbing.

Vision speak is my name for the way Phil prefers to impart information to me. They use my natural ability to visualize. I have always had a big imagination and enjoy my fantasies as mental fun. The Silva Method uses guided imagery to help teach the mind expansion process. It helps focus the mind.

Prior to Silva my fantasies were not always clear. After Silva any created imagery became crisp and clear, very precise and colorful in my mind's eye. Once again, all my practiced efforts could only have produced better results.

When I first started seeing spontaneous visions, those not created by me, they were behind my closed eyes at alpha level or meditation. I would watch them unfold as if watching a short film clip. And then, the visions started showing up on my visual screen when my eyes were open. They would flash information in picture form.

These were never casual visions. There was always information communicated. That was the point of them. Eventually I could walk around with an active vision without disturbing what I was doing. The one main ingredient was that I be in an expanded state, which, by that time I was in most of my waking hours.

Chapter Seven

Spirit and Resolution

Several weeks into my study with Dr. James I asked him to hold out his hand so that I could show him how to play with the electromagnetic field of the body. I had discovered that it is easy to actually feel the body's energy field and use it as an emotional barometer. When we are happy our energy fields extend far out from our physical bodies. When we are sad or depressed the energy field is contracted close to the body. If you have ever run into a bipolar person during a manic phase, the energy field is so large as to be charismatic.

Dr. James declined to play and would not extend his hand. His refusal was surprising and hurt my feeling. I had come to accept him as a friend and his refusal felt like rejection of our friendship.

I left the session feeling dejected. Since I had not eaten all day and was awash in caffeine, I decided to swing into the neighborhood deli for a sandwich on the way home. I needed food to ground me. After two bites into the sandwich I started to choke and cry. I knew I had to get out of there before I made a fool of myself. And that damned vision was pushing itself at me again. This time the BBs were pouring out between the fingers of that hand. The hand was unable to contain them. I went into full panic mode, shaking, sweating, the whole works.

I fled the deli and made a mad dash for the house. As I rushed into the kitchen I glanced at the clock to see how much time I had before my children come home from school. The clock told me I had 45 minutes to get myself together so I would not frighten my beautiful children when they came chattering through the door, filled with the excitement of their day.

I flung myself into a meditative position in my favorite chair and cried out for help. Immediately there was a vision of the interior of a large room filled with rows of chairs. I saw myself standing in the back, facing toward what looked like an altar. How did I know that this was Dr. James' place of worship?

I was fully engaged within the vision now, as the hand began to gently press me to sit in the last row of chairs. I flat out refused. No power on earth could compel me to sit down in that church. Nope, no way. I simply declined the invitation. My fear was that, once again, I would be held captive by a religious philosophy that I found restrictive. I would have to give up my freedom to pursue a spiritual path that had come to mean truth and light and esoteric knowledge, a path that made me happy and excited about my life.

Ever so gently the hand kept encouraging me to sit. I became infuriated and started to verbalize my resistance. With no relief from the vision, I started to scream; really scream, to the cypress rafters in the ceiling. Head thrown back, belly deep, gut wrenching, primal screams, "NO! NO! NO!" God only knows how long that went on. I gave no thought to the neighbors or anyone who might have been walking past the house, wondering if murder was being committed.

Dr. James had invited me to attend his church services. And I had politely begged off. But here I was being urged to do something against my will from an aspect of my Higher Self that I had come to trust. I had flowed along these past months, in a loving and peaceful way for the most part, being gently led by Phil towards higher truths. It had been earthly heaven.

But I had not realized how much of *MY* will, *MY* narrow point of view, was involved. It was okay to expand spiritually as long as we didn't upset the status quo, the closed minded, entrenched belief system I had firmly in place. But Phil deemed it was time to get down to the *real* business of spiritual growth. And after all, hadn't I *asked* for it?

I had actually said to Phil "I'm ready for a change." And they had replied, "Okay, how adventurous are you?"

Continuing to resist the ever persistent vision as it now forcefully pushed me towards the church pew, I dug in with all my emotional might, screaming and cursing at the top of my lungs. My throat was so tight and dry I started to choke. I fought with every ounce of mental, physical and emotional strength I possessed. It felt as if someone had an arm down my throat yanking me inside out like a sock out of the laundry. I was not about to turn over my will to anything, higher or not. It was the most strenuous and emotionally exhausting psychological battled I ever waged in my life. I did not win it.

After what felt like a hours of screaming, I finally threw in the towel out of sheer exhaustion. But as soon as I surrendered and allowed that hand to lead me to the chair it was over. Taking stock of myself. I found that I was soaking wet, breathing in gulps and completely spent.

Somehow, I was still upright in my meditation chair. That in itself was amazing. But then I became aware of a field of energy that surrounded my shoulders. This energy appeared to be holding me upright, like a pair of comforting arms. The written words here will miserably fail to describe just how this energy felt. Words like pure love, profound bliss, home... home, in every sense of the word. I was held in God's love and I was home. It was all that and so much more. It was a Spiritual Presence.

Contemplating the Presence that surrounded me and what I had just experienced, I began to laugh. Light headed and giddy, feeling safe and cherished, I felt like I could float up to the ceiling like a balloon full of helium. I had no weight, no physical restrictions. I had shed some invisible boundary, like gravity, to become air, gossamer. And what is more, I had survived my little tour of hell. I had released the grip of ego and repressed fears and entered some spiritual space of emotional freedom I could not even begin to define. I just knew it was totally safe.

When I felt able to stand, I got to my feet and started across the living room, the Presence still hugging my shoulders. I had not taken more than a few steps when I flashed another vision. It appeared on my visual screen at 12:00 o'clock and conveyed the meaning and understanding of the constructs of Time, its illusions, and how it benefits us in physical reality. All this in a split second.

At 11:00 o'clock I absorbed (no other word for it) how we create physical reality, both actively and passively. At 10:00 o'clock I "got" the illusion of physical reality. At 9:00 o'clock the feelings of Onenes and the understanding of Consciousness (God's Mind) flowed through me; At 8:00 o'clock I began to sense or feel my multidimensional self and understood that what I was experiencing was the integration of body, mind and spirit at a conscious level.

In rapid fire succession, at every hour of the clock, I was receiving esoteric knowledge of how our physical reality works from the non-physical blueprint to the physical manifestation. Right on the heels of that realization was the understanding that ALL I had received was available for anyone to access. It's there for all of us. And yes, there is a much easier way to get it!

Without the Presence to sustain me there was no way I could have remained on my feet. And I had wondered just how far opening to the higher realms of consciousness could go. I had my answer. There is no limit. Even with what I was being taught, I fully understood that it was just a tiny peek into what is available through the intelligence of our Divine Source.

When I came full circle on my visual clock, I wobbled off towards the stairs to the bedroom. Midway up the stairs I felt dizzy and as I grasped the banister to steady myself, the Presence spoke to me very clearly, in a linear fashion,saying, "You will never again have anything to fear, for you will always be protected by the laws that govern nature. You have work to do. There is yet much to learn. What you have witnessed is but a small reward for allowing your integration with Higher Consciousness."

Work! I had more work to do!? I felt like I had just fought world war III and there was more for me to do? As this was running through my mind I sensed the amusement of the Presence. "Yes, you have more work to do, my Shining One, but you do not have to do it all today."

Meanwhile, back at the ranch...

when the children arrived home that day their mother was once again "sane" and able to dispense hugs and cookies. There had even been time to comb my hair and change into dry clothing. What had felt like hours had taken only a few minutes! Time had worked its eternal and magical essence once again.

Chapter Eight

Spirit and Mission

My approach to daily life continued to change and expand. The Presence and I went to check out Dr. James' church the next Sunday. Why wasn't I surprised that the interior was just as I had envisioned? I took the seat where I had been encouraged to sit in my vision.

During the service I understood why Dr. James was never surprised by any of my visions, voices, etc. His was a church of the Christian Charismatic movement. They *all* saw visions and were encouraged to do so. They also spoke in tongues, strange utterances that, they claimed, came from the Holy Spirit. This was an apostolic tradition handed down on Pentecost when the Holy Spirit descended on the twelve apostles and they began to speak in tongues.

After an initial prayer for guidance from the Holy Spirit, service commenced with the singing of original music, composed by members of the congregation, and accompanied by every musical contrivance imaginable. I saw brass, woodwind, percussion and stringed instruments, tamborines, accordions, even spoons. And there was one lovely lady, with a remarkably clear and beautiful soprano voice, playing a small electric organ. It was enjoyable, melodic music, and certainly very lively and uplifting. A happier collection of people praising the Lord you could never encounter.

There was no minister. I was told it was more like a co-op of professional and well educated people who had come together to express their own particular approach to praising God. Individuals got up and spoke or shared some insight or anecdote. If one was led to read a bit of scripture it was read aloud and open to discussion. There was no urgency to get up front, every participant had a natural segue. No one was boring or sanctimonious. There was as much intellectual stimulation as there was emotional and spiritual. I was delighted to note that all seemed have a good sense of humor. These were happy people.

The most interesting aspect of the service was that it seemed to have a central theme, though nothing was rehearsed or planned. This collection of people decided early on to trust the Holy Spirit to lead the congregation in a spiritually pertinent and beneficial program. I had a wonderful time and was surprised to find that the service had taken four hours!

After the service Dr. James introduced me to his wife. She was that lovely lady who played the organ. When I praised her voice she told me she had just returned from the Orient where she had been on tour with a choral group. It was easy to see why Dr. James considered her his soul mate.

They had two precious little blond daughters full of energy and giggles who grabbed my hands and led me all over the hall to meet people. One member told me that she had had a vision of my heart being stretched. My reaction to that was a silent, *"Oh please, give me a break."*

Why was I so unwilling to accept her vision as valid? I certainly had enough experience to know that kind of information was available to anyone who sought it, and even some who didn't seek it. Here in this little church of Charismatics all were encouraged to open and expand their intuitive abilities and trust their visions. They believed this spiritual expansion would lead them to a more meaningful life and a profound union with their Creator. In order to examine and satisfy their spiritual longings, they had formed a loving and accepting community of like minded people.

Though their church was small, the Charismatic movement was huge at that time. I attended a weekend convention at the Miami Convention Center that year. The place was overflowing and out the doors with members just from Florida.

Since I was still unwilling to share that I was seeing visions (my family wasn't even aware of it) this gave me a safe place to further grow and investigate without fear of ridicule. This was my reward for releasing control to Higher Self. But there was also consequence. I had the Presence who had further tricks up ITS spiritual sleeve.

Back on campus fellow students were unaware that they were being seduced by a subtle energetic Presence. I found it vastly annoying. They invaded my space when I was seeking solitude to better commune with my new loving Spirit. More than once I was just quietly sitting, surrounded by acres of campus, when a student or three would approach and ask if he/she/they might join me. Perhaps not a word would be spoken, (and I found this preferable to the ones who wanted to chat) and we would sit in companionable silence. I went from being annoyed to amused to amazed.

The Presence was so powerfully loving and attractive it was a virtual magnet. I knew that this special energy was an aspect of our Divine Oneness. But it felt so different from my normal physical self. And the Presence seemed to have an agenda of ITS own that I was not privy to until events were placed in my path.

One of the classmates in my study group had remarked on the differences in my attitude and manner. Trying to be diplomatic, I'm sure, he kept asking if I was taking anything. I assured him, laughing, that I was not *on* anything, that I had just been doing some intense meditations.

Taking a stroll with me, he started several times to ask me something, stopped and finally blurted out, "Would you put your hand on my solar plexus?"

I wasn't sure where he was going with this request, but I did as he asked. He then placed his hand over mine and after a minute or so, tears filled his eyes. He took a deep breath and said to me, "Thank you. You have just relieved a painful anxiety knot I've been dealing with for months."

"Really? I don't think it was anything I did." It dawned on me that the Presence was at the bottom of this. Healing must be one of Its qualities. I wondered what gave my friend the idea to even ask for a healing. Hummmm…

Many times the Presence would ask me to deliver a message to someone, and usually someone I didn't know. I resisted this little activity because it was too crazy even for me. The messages would be mundane sorts of things, nothing noteworthy or earth shaking that I could see.

It would go something like this: The Presence would focus my attention on someone and communicate, "See that person over there? I want you to go say this (insert message) to him/her."

I would start digging in with my mental resistance, *Nope, not going to do it. That's just plumb crazy. I don't even know that person.*

Synchronicity would then come into play and arrange circumstances so that I would naturally and easily find myself seated next to the person in question. This in itself never ceased to amaze me. I could then casually drop into the conversation and deliver the goods.

That these messages were important to that specific person was readily apparent. I would see a thunderstruck expression, my hand might be grabbed with enthusiasm; I would be thanked profusely, hugged, cried on, all for messages that seemed so ordinary as to be boring.

I reasoned that they must contain code or some hidden meaning. Perplexed, I even wondered if I actually heard something different from what I said. Had I delivered a truly private message meant only for the ears of the one intended?

With a long weekend coming up, which left me free from family and school, I invited one of my northern friends to come enjoy the sunshine and warmth of Florida. I was so looking forward to her visit. She and I shared an interest in the various philosophies and religions of the world, and I thought she would be the perfect person with whom to share my journey. Perhaps she could shed some light on this messaging business.

She arrived full of excitement about a group in town she was currently involved with that espoused the teachings of Saint Germaine. The group was getting ready to burrow into the Earth until such time as they were lifted off into the Heavens.

How do people come to this kind of thinking? I had some knowledge of Saint Germaine but not teachings.

We sat up late into the night discussing this. She was thoroughly convinced the world was in dire trouble from wickedness and bad management and the faithful were to be united with God in a massive evacuation called The Rapture.

With my open and expanded consciousness, I could not begin to tune into this negative belief system she had going. I tried to share some of my experiences with her but she would not hear them. She seemed devoted to leaving the Earth plane.

I suppose, in some ways, my new perspective on reality was no more outrageous than hers. But there seemed something dark about where she found herself.

I awoke the next morning feeling very expanded and with a strong, palpable energy surrounding me. I don't know where it came from but it was not familiar and different from the Presence. It wasn't unpleasant but it was rather confining like a force field.

I walked into the kitchen to find my friend ready to leave for her meeting with the St. Germaine group. When I approached her the energy around me became so strong I could not close the gap between us. My intention had been to give her a hug to take her on her way. Try as I might, all I succeeded in doing was backing the poor woman up again the kitchen counter. I could not get near her. The look on her face was incredulous. Mine must have been as well. I finally had to back out of the room so she could be released to leave the house.

The energy softened but did not dissipate when she left. I could not imagine what that whole scene was about. Strange, to put it mildly. I performed a few breathing exercises and asked the energy to introduce itself. Nothing...

I asked Phil for an explanation. No response.

Feeling the need for food to ground myself but not willing to do the cooking I left for breakfast at one of our local pancake houses.

Sausage, eggs, and pancakes ought to do it; rib sticking and yummy....

Sitting by the window, waiting for my breakfast I felt the energy lift and I was once again "alone."

Why would anyone want to leave this delicious planet? I love it here. The beauty that surrounds me is uplifting; the people engaging and fascinating. Nature is forever entertaining.

To me physical reality was too full of wonder and excitement to ever consider leaving it.

With these thoughts running through my head I had to smile. I was not so naive as to think everyone lived in la-la land as I did. But my friend had everything going for her as far as I could see. She seemed to have a thoroughly successful life. And yet, she had chosen to associate with a group of individuals who wanted to give their lives away.

I felt something tickle the back of my head, and turning to see what it was, I saw, through the large windows, the box hedge that framed the side of the building. It was alive with tiny sparkling lights, flickering and dancing along the top of the greenery.

I sat mesmerized by the light show, thoroughly entertained. The Being that had been "visiting" me was communicating.

"It's so simple. These people are not having a good time. They are only living half a life by being so focused on the negative and ignoring all the gloriousity the material dimension has to offer. They think there is something better waiting for them elsewhere. What they do not realize is that they take their negative beliefs and attitudes with them where ever they go."

My response was, "They think they are bound for Heaven to be with God. Maybe that *is* a better place for some."

"How can any soul *not* be with God. God is everywhere, all that is, all encompassing, at all times. You know that. Your intent to know God has brought you to a communion with Source in many of Its manifestations and allowed you this marvelous existence."

"Can I help my friend?"

"No. For the meantime, this road she is traveling is her choice and giving her life spiritual meaning. She will come to know God in due time. as we all do. It is inevitable."

And with that the lights dimmed and winked out. The energy had left the building. What was it? Where did it come from? I wish I knew. I only know that while it was with me, the Presence had retreated.

I'm glad to say that I was able to enjoy the rest of the weekend with my friend without any further influence from an outside source. Neither of us ever mentioned what had happened in the kitchen.

We had many lively discussions regarding our spiritual lives. She was fascinated by the idea of being a messenger for the nonphysical world, though she had no idea how to explain it.

What *was* going on? Even after all these years I'm still not sure what I was actually doing. I met a fellow metaphysical traveler years later in Connecticut who had a similar experience for several years. He told me that in opening to the will of Source we give permission to be utilized as angels on earth. We were God's messengers for those who sincerely pray for help but have not developed the capacity to hear their Higher Guidance. In prayer we are speaking to God/Spirit, usually asking for something. In meditation we are listening to God/Spirit, hopefully receiving the help we need.

During his angel days he was globe-trotting all over the world with his career as a fashion photographer, so he became an international angel. Most of the time he couldn't see that his messages were anything monumental either, though he did feel like he was doing special work. He gave this warning for any would be angels, "Be prepared to be on call at all hours. The higher realms never sleep and think nothing of directing you anywhere, any time."

Apparently, between his job and delivering messages he was "run ragged," and came home to lay down his angel mission. Though I am not convinced that is what I was doing, it is a sweet explanation.

As a funny aside to this angel business, when there is a message to be delivered it will be delivered. But I had made a determination to stop being Western Union for the Higher Realms. It was while I was enjoying lunch with a good friend, listening to her speak about her new metaphysical way of dealing with things, I had a strong urge to tell her to stop being so verbally open about her new beliefs. It was not serving her beneficially in her present situation. I squelched the urge many times during lunch, often pressing my lips together to keep my mouth shut.

Finally the lunch was over and I was hugging her goodbye. I was so busy congratulating myself on my restraint I let my mind relax. I got halfway to the car, my mind off in space, and without thinking, turned around and walked right back to her and delivered the message! My mouth just opened of its own volition and out came the words. Apparently I can't be trusted to keep my mouth shut. We both had a good laugh about it when I explained to her that I had tried hard all through lunch *not* to give her that message.

As I was walking back to my car I heard, "Pay better attention."

Chapter Nine

Spirit Communicates

Perhaps this is a good time to say something about communication with Higher Guidance, Higher Self, The Guides or whatever we decide to call our non-physical aspect. There can be a difference in levels or dimensions of communication. Each dimension has a resonance and can often be given a name by the one receiving the information.

Those receiving or channeling The Archangel Michael, or the Virgin Mary, Jesus or Mohammed usually came from a religious background and find these names comforting. There is no doubt that receiving communication from what appears to be an outside source has major impact on the one receiving. If it is positive in nature the receiver is generally uplifted by it and may deem it Holy in source. If the communication is not uplifting it is probably being interpreted through a fear based belief system.

Basically all communication comes from the same reservoir of information available to anyone who has reached that level of resonance and intent. And it might be that the level of resonance is determined by the belief systems and natural abilities of the receiver.

There are some communicators who consider their information more authoritative if accompanied by the name of an impressive personality. Myself, I think giving our "informants" a name, any name, makes the communication more personal.

How do we know we are receiving information from a Higher Source? I can only answer for me that it feels very different from my usual way of thinking or answering my own mental questions. My communications are accompanied by a release of endorphins. It feels really good to be tuned into Higher Guidance or in alignment with Source Energy. I am energized by it. If Phil is communicating with words, they use vocabulary I wouldn't normally use.

I asked them once, "What am I?" Their answer was a visual image of a huge, many branched and leafy tree. "You are the outer most leaf on the tree of life, an energy investment cast forth into the physical from Source."

I can tell you I would not think of myself or anything physical as an "energy investment." Besides, I wanted to be a lot more important than the outer most leaf on a big tree. Of course it is those outer most leaves that nourish the Whole. Abraham calls it "the leading edge."

Another occasion I asked again, "What am I?"

Phil's reply - a vision of the Tree of Life began to form on my visual screen.

Please, not the tree again...

"Yes! Look at it. You see a tree with branches and leaves, its trunk with roots into the soil. But it is so much more than that. It is a glorious metaphor for sacred creativity, the beauty and simplicity of which is just stunning. But take a closer look and really perceive what makes up that tree. It is not only leaves and branches, those features which are seen by the physical eyes. What goes on behind its many aspects? What nourishes the tree? What keeps it living? What impact does it have upon its environment?

"Every tiny facet, every leaf of that tree services the Whole. And when such time as the smallest, most seemingly insignificant element has offered all it can in service, it is released to express another aspect *of* the Whole, *for* the Whole. It becomes part of the nutrients of the soil that nourish the tree. It is an unrelenting, sacred dance of creativity, no part of which is inconsequential."

When the Tree of Life metaphor was downloaded it came as one big PDF file (to borrow another metaphor). I had to scramble to get it down in my journal before I lost the salient points and I still did not get it all.

If Phil is communicating through visions without explanation it is up to me to interpret what I am seeing. And that, of course, is determined by my beliefs and unique perspective.

Case in point: years later, sitting with a client in counseling I was smacked with a vision only of an arrow slicing into a man's shoulder. I asked the client if he was having trouble with his shoulder; to which he answered, "Yes. How did you know? I have a damaged rotator cuff that is scheduled for surgery It's very painful."

Since I am not a medical intuitive I had no way of knowing if the arrow signified pain or was a metaphor for another type of issue or if it even applied to the client. I just know that an arrow in my shoulder would be very painful.

But further information suggested his injured left shoulder was indicating his issues with receiving love.

I do not like to read for other people because I'm afraid of the self fulfilling prophesy thing. Why put ideas into anyone's head because they trust you to give them pertinent information. But every once in a while it is forced upon you.

A good friend called one morning while I was meditating and insisted I give her some information on why her son was dressing Goth, associating with undesirable characters and generally making the family life at home difficult.

I explained to her," I don't really do readings. You know that. Please don't ask me to. How would I know if it is the right information for you or him. What if it is something you do not want to hear?"

"Just do it!" she told me emphatically and slammed down the phone. A stressed out mother?

No sooner had the call ended than I was treated to an image of her son, who happened to be one of my favorite young people, decked out in his Goth weeds and looking totally happy. The information came in loud and clear.

"This young man has a learning disability in a family of highly intelligent, highly achieving siblings. His Goth association gives him an opportunity to be accepted and achieve status in a way that is stress free and very easy for him. All he has to do is use his innate creativity expressed as costume. He doesn't have to worry that he is disappointing his peer group or family."

When I gave this information to his mother her response was," My God, I had no idea it was our parental expectations that were having such a negative impact on the whole family."

I started out calling my higher information, The Guides or The Guys and finally Phil. When the Guides/Phil first showed up I was not entirely accepting, and did not trust the information I was receiving. It was such a departure from the usual ramblings of my physical mind.

Where Phil fits in the order of things has often been a cause for interesting questions and dialogue. But time and again their information has proved invaluable. However, I never accept any extraordinary information without a healthy dose of scrutiny, and never without asking for it to be clothed in the Light. Higher Guidance would never ask us to harm anyone or anything.

If you decide to consult a *genuine* communicator keep in mind all information will be presented in a positive manner and **all information is only as clear as the person receiving it, as it will be filtered through the channel's personal perspective and belief systems.** How clear is your communicator? My advice would be to know the person you have chosen to give you sensitive information. And the key to accepting its goodness is how the body reacts to the information. When I hear something important my whole body reacts to it. I *know* it's something I need to consider.

There is also a lower level resonance of the Astral plane inhabited by the newly deceased and confused souls that try very hard to communicate. Be very careful with this information. Often these souls are not aware they have passed on. They want so badly to communicate that they will tell us what we most want to hear. If someone is channeling the recently departed, don't expect to hear anything accurate other than information that person may have had while alive. **Being dead does not open the Akashic records for a soul unless there was a resonance there to begin with.**

Science tells that all creation, physical and non-physical, vibrates at certain frequencies. It stands to reason that communication has its various frequencies as well. Phil has said we can only associate with those frequencies *comfortably* (this is the operative word) if we have resonance. You have heard, "Like attracts like." That is the Law of Attraction. Thank you again, Abraham.

So where did the Presence come from? What was It? It amazes me that in all the time It was with me I never thought to ask It directly. Because I was so comfortable with the energy of It and felt so loved and protected by It, I did not consider It part of me.

At that time I was still floundering in the duality of space/time. Phil had alluded to the Oneness of All and I had experienced glimpses of it, but I still did not get that the Oneness is actually me, actually *all* of us. I felt that I was a visitor to the Oneness since I "came and went." What was happening was that I was allowing a conscious vibrational resonance with Source, or rather aligning with Source. I was coming home for short visits. Staying home would have meant leaving the physical plane all together.

So, at that time, I thought the Presence represented a greater perspective, a better view. Rather like It was standing on the mountain top; Phil was maybe at the mid point scenic lookout and the physical me was mushing along on the valley floor. Together we got the job done.

The Presence did have substance, not physical but energetic. I could sense or feel the essence of It; rather a perceiving with the third eye. I did, in fact, see It a couple of times while in a very expanded state as highly mobile, tiny sparkly flickerings; always associated with lots of loving energy.

Whatever the substance, the emotional impact of the Presence was overwhelming. It filled me up and overflowed around me. It was so attractive to others, in Its subtle way, that people began to relate to me with wide smiles and verbal interaction. They wanted to be close to me. The Presence raised my resonance; I was fine tuned by it, resulting in a blissful state.

When I asked Phil what it was, they replied that it was a collective of Consciousness, a higher resonance, within my Oversoul, "doing ITS thing, with the ability to be consciously aware and present within *all* of Its manifestations." So, a great multi-tasker.

To further explain, Phil said that in the higher realms where all Consciousness merges into the ONE, there is still work to be done. Meaning, the many expressions of Source are ever in a state of Becoming. And where it is necessary, all expressions of the ONE can be called into service. Holy Orders?

I remember my 95 year old mother telling me a week before she passed on that an angel came into her bedroom one night and gave her great comfort. She said she could not remember the exact words but that she finally understood what being One with God meant. She said she was wrapped in so much Love she would never be afraid again. I think that between her fear of transition and her belief in God, she called forth Holy Comfort and It would come to accompany her Home.

Dr. and Mrs. James had another explanation for the Presence. They thought It was the Holy Spirit working through me. It certainly felt holy and it definitely was spirit.

What, after all is the Holy Spirit? In the early days of the evolving, male dominated, Christian church, a group of men got together and decided for all the Christian religions that God had three divine aspects. (how very limiting) The Nicene Creed of 325AD made law that we must believe in the Holy Trinity of Father (masculine/active, [my parenthesis]), Son (created/contracted) and Holy Spirit (ethereal/expanded). During the first ecumenical Council of Nicaea they legislated and removed the personal aspect of spirit, separated physical forever from spirit, and told us there would be no personal relationship between God and man except through the church, its priests and doctrine. And to further insure obedience, they held souls hostage by promising eternity in hell fires if we refused to accept the laws. Wow! And we bought it. No wonder they call it the Dark Ages.

So, getting back to the original question - I'll just get off my soap box now -What is Holy Spirit? I think, and this is my intellectual understanding, Holy Spirit is that aspect of the Divine Creative Principle, the Source of All, that is unlimited possibilities, pregnant with potential. Probably the closest the church fathers were willing to get to a feminine aspect of God. It is that PLACE (for want of a better word) where the blueprint for all things to be manifested into the physical, hangs out.

As for my personal and emotional explanation of Holy Spirit, there are no words to express the knowledge and love that accompany the union of expanded and contracted Consciousness, the marriage of physical with non-physical. That essence of everyone of us is Spirit, is Holy and is Divine.

Chapter Ten

Spirit and Heart

Dr. James had told me in the beginning of our association that his small congregation had initially come together in order to emigrate to Canada to found a center for spiritual advancement within the Charismatic movement. The last Sunday I attended the church was the final gathering of the group before they left the US.

It was a subdued group that assembled that Sunday. Not the usual joyous energy but a quiet, inner reflective mood was settling in and filling the room. Not so surprising since the group was leaving behind friends, some even family, and all their professional lives. I think it took tremendous courage to honor the commitment they had made to their spiritual advancement.

One of the members stood up to say that they were going let the Holy Spirit lead the community to closure with this present church. And that we should all be moved to experience whatever direction that took. No music, no words followed that announcement.

In a few minutes I began to feel an energy moving about the room. I knew I was not the only one to feel it because I heard many clearing their throats, sniffling, shifting of positions, a few whispers. I felt Spirit move through the room as if to touch each one of us, subtle as first, and then becoming strong and purposeful.

All at once, like thunder in my head, it became clear to me just what direction the Holy Spirit was taking. I was frankly dismayed. No, I was appalled.

I started shaking my head, no way. Here I was again, digging in with my most determined mental resistance. But Spirit was strong and issuing an insistent invitation.

I can't really explain how my feet just got up, even with my determination to stay seated. They seemed to develop a life of their own. The Holy Spirit was calling, loud and clear for ITS *own* to come up front, kneel down and accept ITS blessing for the closing of the church and the forthcoming program for Spiritual growth in Canada. This was, after all, a congregation dedicated to Holy Spirit and had placed its trust firmly within.

I was practically in tears from embarrassment. This was just the kind of thing I hated, an open display of religious emotion. I did NOT want to do this but my betraying feet were out of the chair and practically running down the aisle towards the altar. I couldn't stop them.

In the seconds it took me to reach the altar I cannot tell you all of the fearful, funny, and arrogant thoughts that ran through my mind. Upper most were, *"What if I'm the only one up there? Maybe everyone's eyes are closed. Thank God, none of my friends are here to witness this."*

Reaching the altar, I fell to my knees and was immediately overwhelmed by the most profound peace and love. I was blessed with these words from the Presence, "Henceforth, my Beautiful One, you may praise the Lord in any manner you find acceptable."

My puny words cannot possibly express the impact of this blessing. This loving and liberating gift was the last piece. It was my release from past religious conditioning and fears of hell, so ingrained in my Catholic heritage and buried so deep in my psyche, that I wasn't even aware of them. A gift that gave me permission to openly love and express God, to be emotionally involved with my spiritual essence, to honor all forms of religious and spiritual ritual, and foremost, to choose my own way. The Creator, God, ALL THAT IS, in ITS loving wisdom, gives us so many ways to realize our Divinity, it's a wonder that we aren't all running around as enlightened Beings.

I can't say what was experienced by the others at the altar, or if there were, in fact, others there. I saw nothing. I just felt bliss. I think this is what is meant by being reborn. I floated back to my seat, unaware of anything but my communion with the Presence. Whatever time passed after that I couldn't say. I was lost in a joyous sense of adventure and expectation of things to come, with no idea where this new feeling of freedom would lead.

It was a very sad parting when the Jameses left for Canada. Their departure would leave a big hole in my heart. They invited me to come along, but I had a path here in Florida with my family and my profession. And now I had received this amazing and glorious freedom to Be.

Since the summer was fast approaching, and the children anticipating wilderness camp, I would soon be free to put away books and papers, along with left brain consciousness and indulge myself in expanding my intuitive mind and expanded realms of Consciousness.

Chapter Eleven

Spirit and Play

Expanding the mind/consciousness is much like learning anything new. The more you practice, the easier it becomes. The easier it becomes the more you want to practice and the more proficient you can become. I could take a deep breath and expand to where ever I wanted to be. I began to realize that I was in a perpetual altered state of consciousness. I just walked around space/time reality wide open to the energetic vibrations behind it. Everything was more vivid, colorful, interactive. Any questions I had were answered as they formed in my mind or on my lips.

This all started by learning to control my brain waves. Alpha waves are an innate function of the human brain and the natural and first level of the sleep state. Dreams occur in alpha and are necessary to well being. We humans really can function in a more relaxed and more efficient manner with the brain's electrical impulses cycling in the alpha range. It is a much healthier level of consciousness. Research has proven it boosts the immune system, can lower blood pressure, reduce anxiety and cause a sense of well being. But more than that, alpha brain waves can elevate the mind and open the doors to the higher dominions of consciousness, the angelic and Christed realms if you choose to let it. It connects you to the natural world and can enable you to communicate with everything in your physical reality as well. That's what mind expansion is all about. You use much more of the potential of the human brain.

Communicating with the natural world is a lot of fun and can be quite an education. Nature has a delightful sense of humor and is so ready to chat with anyone who will listen. Because nature resonates within the alpha range of vibration, we often find it relaxing and soothing. Taking a walk through your favorite outdoor setting or your own back yard can be one of the most healing things you can do for yourself.

Did you realize that the reason that cut flowers stay fresh and beautiful for a couple of weeks is because their God given vitality is so robust that it takes time for the energy to withdraw? This vital energy, present in all life, actually can communicate, given the opportunity.

I am reminded of one particular instance as a prime example of how lively and playful nature can be. I had tried a new kind of noisy meditation recommended by a fellow student of Yoga. He called it chaotic meditation. I think it is the kind of thing practiced by the Eastern Dervishes. It calls for an undisciplined kind of leaping and spinning while chanting anything that comes to mind. It's quite a workout if you can keep it up for any length of time.

After one very energetic, early morning effort, I left for the supermarket. Let me say, I got in my car and drove to the local farmer's market. I remember that I was mildly surprised to find myself arriving there without having made any prior decision or having any reason to go. I had not even brought my purse.

I walked into the produce section of the market barehanded. I didn't bother taking a cart. At this particular market, the produce was displayed at the front of the building with huge automatic garage type doors open to the parking lot.

Entering, I was immediately faced with a stand of fresh peaches. The color of those peaches was so vibrant that I had to drop my gaze in order to approach them. I was powerfully attracted to them and wanted to touch one. But try as I might, I could not look directly at them. The energy shimmering around them was blinding. Foregoing the peaches, I advanced further into the fruit section and also could NOT look directly at the any citrus, bananas or melons. They were all so vibrant with energy my physical eyes could not behold them.

It wasn't until I reached the cherries that I was able to focus my eyes on the fruit. The cherries were so attractive that I stopped to feast my eyes on them. I could not get enough of their lush, red beauty. As I stood there, transfixed, a lady with a high pitched, screech of a voiced whined, "Oh for God's sake! They're all rotten!"

It was such a jarring note I felt as if my body had been slammed against a wall. I was really glad that she immediately left the produce section. Later I was to consider that perhaps the cherries were past their prime and that's why I *could* look directly at them. I did not experience anything rotten, however.

After I was startled out of my cherry reverie, I glanced up, only to be captivated by the greenery of the broccoli across the aisle. I hope you can appreciate the difficulty I find in trying to assign words to express what was essentially an expanded state of consciousness beyond even words of superlative description. I was enthralled by the broccoli. I walked over to stand in front of a glorious mound of it and was drawn into its profound substance. It was so perfectly, gloriously green. The broccoli was, in a sense, showing off, teasing me with its beauty and vitality.

Time, or no time, was in charge again. After some duration I noticed the lettuces. They were so magnificent that I stood entranced before each mounded variety. I went down a line of artfully arranged vegetables, enraptured, until I reached the mushrooms. There, I was overwhelmed with emotion and burst into tears. I had never seen anything so exquisite as those mushrooms. I put my hands into their skillfully mounded arrangement and let the silky buttons slide through my fingers. I was lost in beauty and time, and fully prepared to spend the rest of my life right there... until I caught movement off to the side and noticed the produce manager coming towards me with a look of concern on his face. *OK, time to leave...*

When I got to my car I just erupted into peals of laughter. I felt giddy and light and full of fun. Phil told me that I had just been treated to what was in store for the future of our race. They called it "true association." We humans will evolve to the point of not having to actually consume our food but to associate with its true essence. We will be nourished by the energy of it. Great way to diet!

Well, let me tell you, it was a long time before I shopped in that market again. And when I did I wore dark glasses and a hat. I laugh every time I think about how I must have looked walking into the market, staring at and crying all over the produce, for who knows how long. That whole morning was lost in earth time to me. I have no memory of eating anything that day.

Was I getting further "out there?" I suppose I was. But I had the perfect reality check in my family. Kids keep your feet on the earth. We all breezed through our days getting ready for summer and camp. The children would remark now and again that I was more fun than I used to be. There was a more relaxed atmosphere in the house since I'd decided not to be perfect, less demands made on my husband. I could not hide the fact that I was different from my usual uptight, over achieving, loquacious self. It does my friends credit that they watched me change into a laid back, happy homemaker with a metaphysical bent and still invited me over for dinner.

My gardens were a continuing source of joy and communication. Just the act of sticking my hands into bedding soil was a peak experience. I grew up in the real Mississippi cotton growing Delta, along the mighty river. I suppose I am just a dirt farmer at heart. So my gardening passion brought happy and edible results for my loved ones.

Never having been a particularly good cook, I prepared basically the same things over and over. Those old tried and true meals that I knew my family would eat with a minimum of coercion, appeared on the table time after time. After a while the family cook became a robot in the kitchen. I could read a book and cook at the same time.

With this new awareness, cooking became an interesting adventure. Harvest brought vegetables and herbs to the table that were initially alien to me but which quickly found their way into exotic, as well as healthful dishes. This all came about because the vitality of food comes equipped with its own intelligence as to the most beneficial way to be prepared. Really! Plants know their way in the world.

Conversations with food…what a spark to gastronomic creativity! I do not want to minimize the importance of this. I had already been treated to the overwhelming vitality presented by the produce we buy for our consumption. The energy that remains within the harvested food not only will, but longs to communicate with us. It is the Divine interaction between all things, physical and non-physical.

There is an awesome intelligence within the Source of All present in all things. There is not one infinitesimal juncture of the multiverse that does not represent some form of intelligence. All it takes is the intent to know it and a quiet mind to access it. This intelligence will communicate on any subject from the simple preparation of a squash timbale to the cure of any and all disease. It will communicate with a sense of fun, humor, and love. And it will probably tell you *more* than you ever wanted to know.

Chapter Twelve

Spirit and Speech

It was during the summer break that the Presence took ITS leave as I was washing dishes one evening - there's just something about immersing my hands in warm, sudsy water that allows my inner self to swing free. When I returned to earth, I realized I had been crying. My face was wet with tears and the front of my shirt was soggy. I knew I had been away but had no memory of where. One thing was immediately obvious. The Presence was gone and I was left with a sense of overwhelming loss.

In my efforts to recall the Presence, I poured more time into meditation. I begged Phil to help me grasp where and why the Presence had gone.

They told me *why* the Presence had gone meant that our work together was complete.

Understanding *where* the Presence had gone was a bit more difficult. The Presence had gone no place, since there is only ONE place, the ONE. But rather, IT had withdrawn ITS attention. IT *de*-focused from our physical aspect. I was an energy investment for specific purpose and had been released to further my earthly journey and physical focus. It was time for me to move on.

My life during that time was full of contentment and supported luxuriously by an empire building husband. It was an interesting space for me, having been so previously goal and ego driven. I would examine my earthly position occasionally, reality checking. I came to the conclusion I was no longer living life, which in the past meant I was chasing after life. Now Life was expressing through me. It was a true partnership between my spiritual and physical selves, a balanced body, mind and spirit.

With the children at camp and my husband involved in work and related travel, I was alone much of the time. Summer in South Florida is a desert of activity. It's even too hot for the beach for any length of time. Everyone who can, clears out for cooler climes. So I was alone to explore the further reaches of my spiritual universe. My companions were the flora and fauna of subtropical South Florida. I had occasional visits with friends as they drifted in and out of town. Actual verbal communication was very minimal.

It is my experience that our species holds in common with all of forms of nature the ability to communicate. This communication is not necessarily verbal nor linear. It can occur telepathically and springs full blown into the mind through thought transfer, thought images, or visions and feelings/emotions. A whole concept can be conveyed in its totality and be so full of information that it is difficult to retrieve every bit of it. Because I had been practicing this kind of non-verbal communication on a regular basis, and found it not only useful but efficient, I relied less and less on my verbal skills. I had no idea this would pose a problem for me down the line.

With my family away, there would be days where I would not verbalize more than a few words. I had basic conversation while shopping, quick talks on the phone. There was nothing that would tax my verbal skills and call for any in-depth thought. My mind was so alive with non-verbal communication that I wasn't aware how little I was actually speaking out loud.

My husband was never a great conversationalist. Prying words out of his mouth got to be a challenge. Friends and family used to tease him about it. He saved his words for the many business meetings and trade shows where public speaking was a necessity. When he was home he craved quiet.

So different from my husband, the children and I were blabber mouths. We all jabbered away at the same time, talking over one another. I had been verbose, even glib before my spiritual awaking. Fortunately for me, I did not need nor desire to engage in deep and meaningful verbal conversation at that time. Verbalizing took too long to get the point across.

I found the absence of chatter, both mentally and verbally, left a clear path to exquisite communication with Source's many physical and non physical expressions. There is so much going on behind the scenes of our very limiting five senses. The Multiverse is alive with amazing expressions of Divine Creation.

My verbal skills began to atrophy; no other word for it. It seemed that my brain was no longer connected to my mouth. The words were just not there. This still remains the most mysterious occurrence of that whole period. What happened to my speech? Perhaps my left brain was taking a much needed nap.

One positive aspect of this was that it must have been a relief for my friends, and especially for my husband, to be granted a break from my long winded opinions.

As summer drew to a tranquil and satisfying close, we all geared up for the activities of fall, work and school. I prepared to resume my internship in Marriage and Family counseling without giving much thought to my more expanded approach to reality. This offered some new and interesting developments.

Prior to the end of last term I had sat in on a few of the private counseling sessions conducted by my adviser and mentor. My job was just to observe and then offer comments and discussion after the session. It was the prerequisite for the actual residency to take place in the fall. I was both excited and anxious about being involved in counseling even though, most of the time, listening is the real key to effective counseling. Good thing, since my speech was at a bare minimum.

By the time of fall residency I had become adept at keeping a calm and relaxed expression while a vision was insinuating itself on my visual screen. With this psychic advantage, I was able to "read" many of the clients. And those with the strongest emotional issues were broadcasting energy the moment they entered the office. Though I never revealed what I sensed or saw while counseling anyone, I was able to discern the deep seated problems within the relationships. This enabled me to ask pertinent questions and help the clients to get to the heart of their relationship issues in a timely manner.

Before each session, I would center and give myself permission to receive any information appropriate for the clients. Though it sometimes spontaneously happened, I did not want to intrude on any facet of their lives not involving their personal relationship. This centering seemed to promote a safe environment for dialogue and exchange of emotions.

Where there were children involved in a counseling session, I noticed that the young ones responded to my energy easily and quickly. It calmed them. The adults, with years of intellectual and emotional conditioning, took a bit longer, but never the less, responded as well.

Initially, I was unaware this exchange of energy was taking place until clients commented on it. It seemed that many entering my office in a negative emotional state left more relaxed, some even happy and continued to be so for about twenty-four hours. This was amusing because I got calls for sessions more often than the usual once a week. Without really thinking about it, I was raising the vibrations in the room and the clients were reaping the benefits.

After several remarks to this effect, I started to pay attention to my energy when clients stepped into the room. I became aware of a subtle vibration, a soft rhythm of influence that moved about the room and interacted with all present. This energy was experienced as calming and pleasant.

Though I do not know exactly how this energy exchange works, I believe this is what we call a contact high. If you have ever been swept along by a person or group of people having a joyful time you will recognize this type of energy transfer immediately. Expanded, happy states are contagious! And so are calm relaxed ones.

Chapter Thirteen

Spirit and Education

Returning to an academic setting brought the frustrating problem of having to relearn learning. I had always relied heavily on my remarkable memory. But gradually, throughout the summer, my memory began releasing most of the useless trivia collected from a lifetime of interests, reading and study. So the acquisition of new information without the benefit of fully functioning, left brain memory and analytics was not only discouraging but down right frightening.

I became very quiet in class, sitting in the back, where previously I had sat up front and participated. Listening to the professor, I seemed to get caught up in the sound of the voice rather than the content of the information. Without reliable memory I would have to take decent notes for the first time. However, I could not take good notes because I got lost trying to spell even the simplest words correctly. It was an interesting as well as alarming situation. Though I was not as driven to excel as before, I still wanted to do well. The tension caused by the situation brought me to tears of frustration. It was not surprising that my adviser finally asked me to meet him after class to discuss any problems I might be having.

Face to face with an authority figure in my chosen field, lacking the verbal skills I once possessed to facilitate explaining my unusual situation, I simply burst into tears. I didn't know where to start. There was so much I didn't understand and was suddenly afraid that the professor would just write me off as another scholastic burnout. Graduate school dropout is legendary. How could I tell a prominent psychologist that I was hearing voices, seeing visions and losing verbal and memory skills? I just mumbled that I was having trouble at home and fled.

For the first time it occurred to me that I might not be able to graduate. And if I wanted a career in psychology I would have to complete classes and write a thesis for a degree. All that time and money down the drain and what was worst, I didn't really seem to care that much any more.

I seemed to have shed my drive to be superwoman during the summer. And isn't that why I went back to school initially? In my centered and spiritually integrated state, the desire to prove self worth, through an intellectual accumulation of knowledge, was no longer necessary. And now I no longer felt the need to save the world. I was totally fulfilled at home with my family and gardens. But I was so close to completion…these were my arguments and mental harangues I heaped on myself until I was ready to scream.

These distressing thoughts took up most of a weekend. I took the conflict to my mental laboratory and consulted Phil. Their advice was to relax in class and not try to take notes; just to listen and allow my psyche to assimilate and synthesize the information. And after all, all information was readily accessible through the pathways of Multiversal Intelligence. They assured me that I would do well on exams. They also said that my expanding senses and experiences would prove a benefit to others when the time came.

Returning to class I felt much more relaxed and ready to get on with the business of getting on. And without the interference of note taking, I actually got more out of the lecture. If I had questions on the subject, the answers seemed to form in my mind before I could verbalize them. I could keep my mouth shut and not dread trying to make speech.

Using the alpha state helps to focus on what is important for the moment and filters out extraneous stimuli. Learning becomes easier and retention is routed to long term memory.

Shortly after the fall term started I got a note asking me to drop by the Anthropology department to meet with a new professor from UC Berkley. Perplexed but very interested, I made an appointment for the following day.

Dr. Brun was a good looking, young hot shot with a new PhD and a million dollar smile. I liked him immediately. He explained that he was researching natural and drug induced altered states in the Native American religious rituals and had gotten permission to form a select group for the class. He had invited ten others and wanted me to be part of the group. One of his grad students was a friend of mine and had suggested that I would be a good participant for the research.

I thought it would be an excellent opportunity to throw a little of the scientific method at my metaphysical and intuitive itinerary in order to help me understand what was happening at an organic level. I think some small part of me still needed assurance that I wasn't just slipping off the edge.

Why wasn't it enough that I felt physically and mentally better, worked more efficiently, had closer and more loving relationships with my friends and family, was more effective in counseling sessions, and certainly had more day to day enjoyment of life?

Funny, huh? I guess a house has to fall on us before we allow ourselves to enjoy life to the fullest. If everything is this good, something must be wrong! Murphy's Law in full bloom.

As I mentioned earlier, the drug culture of the 60s and 70s had struck with a resounding chord. The human sciences were thrown into confusion as to how to explain it, let alone how to deal with it. Anthropologists had studied the psychedelic-induced altered states for years and were comfortable with the reasoning that gifted and practiced Shamen knew how to handle the altered states without causing permanent mental or physical illness. But many of the younger generation, ones who got caught up in the counter-culture after Viet Nam just couldn't handle the explosive and radical mind blowing states caused by the hallucinogenic drugs. It was now time for the sociologists and psychologists to get involved.

There were a few astute scholars in the 60s and 70s who accomplished some excellent research in mind expansion and came to the conclusion that any drug induced, altered state could be replicated with the natural mind. And, according to Dr. Brun, proving *that* was our mission, should we chose to accept it.

Jake, he told us to call him, had invited a cross section of disciplines for his study. The eleven of us represented the sciences of sociology, psychology, philosophy, anthropology, chemistry and the new disciplines of psychopharmacology and ethno-botany. All of us were already familiar with or regularly practiced meditation. And all of us had experienced, at least once, some kind of drug induced altered state in the past, either with alcohol, marijuana or the hallucenogenics. We all considered ourselves professionals in our fields and productive members of society. We did not practice drug use.

The class met once a week for four to five hours in the evening. We asked, and had been granted by the department head, to rotate the sessions through the homes of our classmates. The nature of our focus often needed a comfortable, quiet setting and subdued lighting not offered in the classroom.

Our investigations began by contrasting our normal waking states with the varied meditation and breathing practices of the Eastern philosophies. We then proceeded to explore the breathing techniques of Stanislau Grof, the mind games of Jean Houston, the journals of Carlos Castanedas, and the natural mind of Andrew Weil.

Since this is what the Silva Method had taught me, I was not surprised to find that, to a greater or lesser degree, depending upon the ability of the classmate to relax and trust the process, we all did feel more relaxed, could induce vivid, colorful imagery, and experience the natural, altered states of consciousness.

Though I was relatively new to non-psychological group dynamics at that time, the Silva experience being the exception, one thing became very clear as we progressed.

Shared expanded states of consciousness open the heart. We all fell in love with and trusted one another. In the years since, being the facilitator of many successful groups, I can testify to that. Doing a brief meditation will open a group's dynamics and bring about an honest and loving interaction.

Though there was no quantitative way to measure our expanded states outside of class, we did have a questionnaire provided by Dr. Brun for us to subjectively determine how the expanded states progressed each week. On a scale of one to ten we would determine how we were affected by our altered states. We had each made a promise that, for the duration of the term, we would not partake of any substance that could alter consciousness, accept for mild caffeine. No drinking, smoking, inhaling or chewing of anything considered a drug. Since we did not do that anyway it did not pose a problem for anyone except for one tobacco smoker.

Instances of peak experience, time warp (slowed or accelerated) and the heightening of senses out of the meditative state were reported. Colors seemed brighter, music was more meaningful, touch was more sensitive. The latter provided a real bonus for the sexually active of the group.

I want to reinforce a very important point. Even if you don't meditate or make an effort to relax, anytime we are present in the moment, that is, really paying attention to what is happening right now, the senses are heightened. This is because we have removed the wall of indifference to the moment. It makes life so much more enjoyable. Everything feels new and exciting. I often quote Dan Millman from his book, <u>THE WAY OF THE PEACEFUL WARRIOR,</u> "There are no ordinary moments."

I had several instances of spontaneously being out of body. I can't say I enjoyed the out of body experience (OBE). They would happen while I was sliding into meditation. My astral or non-physical body would lift halfway out of my physical body and just hang there until I either gave up meditation or it lifted off to parts unknown. I would be gone for a while and then feel myself settled back into my physical body. It wasn't until I attended my first workshop at the Monroe Institute years later that I learned how to control the OBEs.

I had not shared any of my heretofore spiritual exploration because I did not want to scare anyone nor influence the outcome of the research. We were, after all, a mentally stable group within the paradigm of academic study with, what we considered, an important premise to prove.

No part of the study was interfering with our abilities to function or perform the tasks of daily living. Quite the contrary. We all agreed that we were actually more effective in our daily lives and that a drink of hard alcohol, a glass of wine or a hit of marijuana was no longer appealing. We were naturally high. And it was a pure high without headaches, munchies or paranoia. If you can imagine college without beer or pot that will give you an idea of how well the mind expansion exercises elevated our senses.

The drug culture of today scares the daylights out of me. I can understand the need to relieve the pain and suffering of those whose lives are fraught with misadventure and misfortune. And on a *short* term basis, some organic substances can show the way to a safer avenue of relief if taken in the proper environment. But the designer drugs are destroyers of body, mind and soul. As far as I can tell they serve only to line the pockets of those greedy, irresponsible purveyors of death who sell them. I see it as a slow, chemical suicide for those who allow themselves to become addicted.

Those in the class who had tried a psychedelic substance lauded the Stanislau Grof Holotropic Breathing techniques as an excellent substitute. This technique calls for a type of steady and controlled breathing, near hyperventilation, for about an hour at first, less time as you become more adept. The breathing takes you through stages of relaxation, then mental expansion and finally into what I call a spiritual lift off.

The exercise takes commitment but is well worth it. It is mentally and physically safer by far than any designer drug. However, the breathing should not be done alone since space and time get mixed up along with the senses. I would recommend reading up on the technique before trying it. It is not recommended for anyone with cardio-vascular problems.

Our first occasion of Holotropic Breathing, after close to an hour of controlled breathing, I felt the need to relieve my bladder. I got lost wondering around in the house in search of a bathroom. (Note: always go before any meditative exercise as the bladder relaxes and distracts from the process)

Everything I looked at along the way captured my attention so thoroughly I could hardly bare to leave it. I had to touch and smell many objects before I could identify them. And moving, I felt as if I were on a skate board. I eventually found the bathroom where I became totally infatuated with my reflection in the mirror. I could not get over how beautiful I looked. There was a soft glow around me that I found captivating. I suspected I was seeing my aura. I found that I could control its size by thinking certain thoughts. The positive thoughts made the aura larger and negative thoughts made it smaller and sometimes changed its color.

I don't know how long I had been standing there playing with my aura when a classmate came looking for me. I immediately saw her aura and pointed it out. I hugged her to me and the auras became a very pretty pulsing rose color. We stood for a while admiring our beautiful and colorful selves and tried to make the energy flow out of our mouths, like inhaling and blowing colorful smoke. When our facial efforts became comical, we then started making silly faces at each other's mirror image. The results were vastly amusing. We ended up laughing so uproariously that Jake heard us from the living room and sent a posse to drag us back to the exercise.

When the others located us in the bathroom, we insisted that they join us in producing a group aura. So everyone crowded into the room and tried to get into a group hug. This proved difficult since the bathroom was not large. If you can visualize a group of adults in a narrow room trying to make a group hug, getting into all kinds of positions so that all were touching and still able to see ourselves in the mirror, you will agree that is cause for humor. However, all of us being in an expanded state, we were over the top laughing.

Thus a second posse was sent. They also were persuaded to join our effort and that resulted in more boisterous behavior, until finally Jake himself came and insisted we come back to the living room. We followed him back like a group of naughty children trying to keep straight faces. Unfortunately that proved to be too much for us and we disrupted the exercise so completely that Jake felt it necessary to verbally discipline us.

We were in no state to take anything seriously and continued to snigger and giggle. You know how it is when you are trying *not* to laugh. Finally the whole group just erupted in to side-splitting laughter so that we, including Jake, gave it up and laid around on the floor for the rest of the evening being silly and laughing hysterically. No one wanted to go home.

During another evening of focused breathing I happened to glance over at a classmate to see, superimposed over her face, a holographic image of an ancient aboriginal woman. It was glowing and appeared to be vibrant. It was so startling to me that I looked away and blinked my eyes several times before I looked back at her again. The image stayed on her face for some time. I could not make it go away by blinking my eyes or shaking my head.

Later, when I told the classmate what I had seen, she informed me that she had been exploring a life spent as an aboriginal shaman. How could she have projected an image that I was able to see? She did tell me she was unaware of what she was doing other than following the trail of thought that was presented to her through her expanded state.

And why am I still surprised when these things happen to me? I shared her vision. Was my consciousness linked with hers? There are so many levels of reality, both physical and non, to explore. And I suppose that deleting the need for logical explanation is helpful. Phil keeps telling me to just enjoy the experiences.

There was no replication of my left brain dysfunction reported by any members of the group. No one described any problems with short term memory loss or aphasia. But then, no one had made so focused an effort to expand their intuitive abilities over a period of months.

Toward the end of the class I did share some of my experiences. No one had knowledge of aphasia outside of stroke victims or those with actual brain trauma or disease. In discussing this we all agreed that there was a good possibility that a prolonged and intense intuitive focus naturally created this kind of right brain dominance. That made sense to me. However, does it necessarily follow that a dominance of either hemisphere of the brain precludes a balanced performance of both? Is it an either or situation?

I think the aphasia could have been forestalled if I had been aware of the possibility that I could lose verbal skills. Perhaps I could have taken measures to redirect it before it became established. But I will reemphasize that verbal communication is ponderous, and can lead to miscommunication, compared to nonverbal communication.

I am convinced that each of us has an unconscious dictionary, motivated by emotions experienced throughout childhood. Many words are emotionally influenced by personal experiences and can be loaded with all kinds of subtext, often to the detriment of communication. Home or love are two such emotionally charged words and will carry far different meaning to one who had an abusive childhood as to one who grew up in a loving environment.

Avram Noam Chomsky, considered the father of modern linguistics, said "Even the interpretation and use of words involves a process of free creation." Doesn't it make you wonder just how much we actually do understand what each of us is trying to communicate? I believe that telepathy is much more efficient as it can convey the emotional impact along with the information.

The encouragement of left brain function by orthodox science and education has created a society largely reliant on logic and reason. I believe that fear of ridicule by our peers has caused distrust of our perceptual awareness and psychic insight with the resulting atrophy of our intuitive proficiency. Surely there is a good and sound reason why our brains encompass both rational and intuitive capability.

Years later, when I attended a weeklong workshop in intuitive communication at The Monroe Institute in Faber, Virginia, I was surprised to find that some members of our group had been sent there by the research and development departments of IBM, I.A. DuPont, Virginia Electric, and the US Army. In fact two of the original participants in the Army's remote viewing research program were living and working there. Big business had come to the conclusion that left brain analytics needs communication with expanded, right brain creativity. It is *not* for nothing that we have two hemispheres to our brains.

In the final analysis it is up to each of us to determine just how much we want to cultivate our innate ability to communicate with the greater, non-physical aspects of ourselves. Perhaps the solution to a better balance of physical and non-physical activity is to constantly exercise both sides of our brains. Memory games and cross word puzzles along with meditation can be excellent activities for balancing the left and right hemispheres. But I have to confess, after years of trying to balance both, it is the spiritual connection that has suffered. Though I am once again comfortable with my analytical, left brain access, I thoroughly miss the instant and persistent communication with the natural world. In those days, I could have picked up a hoe and a packet of seeds and wondered off into the hills without a backward glance.

Chapter Fourteen

Spirit Moves On

As the days progressed, and I continued to expand and integrate within my non-physical aspects, I couldn't help noticing that my relationship with my husband began to change. I certainly was not the person he married. And though he never mentioned my obvious changes, he must have been confounded by them. I had become a quiet, serene, homebody who had quit demanding any emotional feedback from him. After one instance of trying to share my experiences and being told he wasn't interested I never tried again. I think he was just enjoying the peace and quiet that required nothing from him.

It was clear I was very different from the young, unformed person he married. Here, *unformed* is the operative word. So many of us, both male and female, go into marriage/relationships not knowing who we really are, reactive rather than responsive. I believe most women marry because they see the *potential* rather than the spouse. Perhaps we believe we can mold them into the person we believe they can be. What we are actually seeing is the potential within ourselves. Those of us who wake up and begin to grow can become a startling stranger to our significant others if there is no honest communication. Those who manage to grow together are truly blessed.

In the beginning it was my husband who was intrigued by the Silva method. Friends of ours had taken the program and felt they had gained much from it. It helped their personal communication and helped them reduce the stress around raising a dyslexic child.

The four of us had a lively discussion over dinner at our house about two months prior to the next workshop being offered in Fort Lauderdale. I was fascinated by the stories from their workshop experience. My husband decided we should sign up but not take the course together. I went along with his plan and suggested he should go first as I was booked up with school and volunteer work.

I'm not sure what he actually got out of it but fun and a working acceptance of the mind/body connection. He only discussed a few of his experiences with the techniques. As I have said, he just wasn't one for sharing his inner thoughts and feelings. I had hoped the course would at least open him up to a deeper level of communication with me and the children. He did tell me that he thought I would profit a lot from the relaxation exercises. Little did we know...

As a husband, the man was an excellent provider and faithful companion who seldom went out with the guys. He was home every evening at the same time unless he was on one of his many business trips. I considered him my best friend. But he was totally incapable of sharing any emotional depth with me. It wasn't that he didn't have deep feelings, he just did not feel comfortable sharing them. Maybe it's a guy thing.

I demanded a level of intimacy that he just refused to allow. And truthfully, his real love was the business that he and his family were very successfully growing into an international company. The children and I were always competing with the company for his attention. Those of you who are married to an overachieving spouse will recognize this scenario. It must have been a tremendous relief to him when I focused my emotional needs elsewhere.

My evolving spiritual connection helped me to understand that my emotional demands had been masks for feelings of inadequacy. I needed my husband to love me enough for both of us. I was not in touch with my own worth and was trying to fill that void by looking outside myself for validation.

And it wasn't just my husband I depended upon for this approval. My sense of self was totally tied up in successful accomplishmen - mother, wife, homemaker, my education, career, civic volunteering. All of the tremendous amount of energy I expended was directed outward to show the world that I was a worthy and valuable person. But somewhere lodged within all that effort was a very satisfying feeling of exploring my own excellence. I don't want to minimize that. I could, after all, get the job done. And in those days, what I *did* was who I thought myself to be.

Phil, with more on the subject, offered, "You limit yourself by identifying with what you do. You are neither the action nor the behaviors that accompany it. You are far more than that. Action is a form of entertainment you choose to amuse yourselves. Action is a gift of the physical plane and blessed by Spirit."

With this new and wonderfully light centered sense of Being, I had passed another milestone in spiritual/emotional growth. I no longer needed to demand emotional satisfaction or a sense of worth from the people and world around me. I had discovered the source of it within.

I found it amazing how effortless my time became when I chose to accept those opportunities that truly expressed my new state of Being. And I could continue to take pleasure from my efforts for the joy and creativity alone.

Being spiritually expanded is a healthy, robust state. There is nothing fragile about an open psychic channel. Spirit is so seductive, so warm and cozy and loving that it is easy to stay in a blissful state. If I had known I could balance the spiritual and physical I might have chosen to remained an open channel. But maybe it was just time to return to a more physical focus. There was a tug in that direction. And Phil did say I had more work to do.

Apparently there is *always* more work or evolving and growing to do no matter whether you're physically, emotionally, mentally or spiritually focused. It never ends, even in the nonphysical. Get used to it.

Phil told me once, "You are ever quivering on the threshold of your potential. Creation IS a state of Becoming and you are an integral part of that."

So, with children, hearth and home, I knew that I would have to coax my left brain functions into some semblance of performance. I was determined to be normal again... whatever that meant. I made myself communicate verbally, which was often cause for hilarity. Frequently words and mouth did not match up. I shut myself off to any free floating emotions upon entering a room. I played memory games with myself.

It was slow going, but with the effort came good results. While I seldom see unwanted, spontaneous visions, I can still access the expanded realms of consciousness for guidance, while accomplishing a day full of business. I can perform analytical tasks and communicate with nature and Phil whenever I actively choose. I have an ongoing, daily dialogue with Phil and my environment which is a never ending source of amusement as well as instructive. I strive daily to achieve a physical and spiritual balance that allows me the freedom to create a wonderfully meaningful, abundant life full of creative expression. And this has served me well.

As I began to feel comfortable with the balancing of my spiritual and physical realities I was able to understand that the spiritual or nonphysical aspect of me was actually the blueprint of my physicality. All physical manifestation has first a vibrational blueprint, just like any architectural reality has before construction begins. It is first an idea, then a series of drawings, perhaps a model and finally a physical actuality.

Phil had explained that every aspect of creation is energetic vibration. The rate at which its expression vibrates determines how manifested or physically real it appears. This ever present, free flowing energy is the stuff of creation. Phil calls it the Creative Principle.

Because I was willing to entertain the thought of actually becoming a conscious creator as the author of the life I wanted to live, interesting and often amazing people, circumstances and events began to manifest in my physical reality. And because I was conscious of what I was allowing through that energetic or spiritual aspect of myself, I was aware - and awareness is vastly important to quality of life -I was aware of what I was causing to happen. And I was determined that it be positive and beneficial to me and those around me.

"This is conscious living," Phil informed me. "Your approach to life and decision making is responsive, based on preference, joy, love, rather than reactive or fear based. Express yourself through your talents and creativity. You can only attract that which is essentially you. Pay Attention; Know Thyself; Love Thyself, and allow the world come to you."

Part Two

Living Consciously

Chapter Fifteen

My husband and I divorced the year following school. It was difficult for all of us in spite of the ease of the legalities. I think I cried for the first two years thereafter every time I was around the children's father. And that was often as we both felt the children needed us to support each other as parents.

I felt so guilty and took full responsibility for the split up. But without dialogue and an emotional sharing I could not continue in the relationship, though I knew he would have. Looking back, I believe that he felt that I was doing such a good job of maintaining the home front that he was free to express his excellence in building the family business. I wish I had understood that then.

The children and I stayed in the house while their father moved close enough for them to abandon the mother ship for his place when I was serving a dinner they didn't care to eat. I think we continued to be good parents. And he seemed to be more available to the children from around the block than he ever was at home.

I became a certified Marriage and Family Counselor and set up offices in both Miami, to help a colleague out a couple of evenings a week, and in Fort Lauderdale, just down the street from our house. Along with private counseling I had many successful workshops, three of which were acknowledged in the Miami Herald newspaper. Keeping spiritually open and centered I was able to provide a safe environment for honest, emotional expression, whether individually or in group.

During this time I was learning the art of living consciously. That is, I was becoming more and more aware of the nuances of physical reality as a mirror for the greater nonphysical aspects of creation. This was often brought home to me through the couples I was counseling. Though they initially had difficulty accepting the concept of the other as a mirror, it proved useful and healing as they began to gain insight and grow emotionally.

Phil told me that our significant others are the most important relationships we have for spiritual and emotional growth. And a significant other can be a spouse, a lover, a pet or a house plant. Our behaviors, thoughts and feelings, in relation to that other, holds all the clues to our emotional and spiritual growth. Acknowledging that, I found there was no going back to the old way of understanding or deciphering life. It was a whole new way of being physically focused with a unique perspective.

Phil further explained, "You actually *are* your reality, everything and everyone in it. If you want to know yourself, thoughts and beliefs, take a look at the reality you have created. All the clues are there."

A prime example of this came to roost on my shoulders years later when I almost lost my beloved best friend, my dog Rebel. It started with his gradual decline from a happy, energetic dog to his depression and loss of mobility.

As he became less and less mobile I had to carry him outside for his business. But after many veterinary visits with tests and x-rays, the vet could find nothing wrong with him.

Desperate, I took Rebel to a healer who stretched him out on her message table and went over him with her energy reading. Her diagnosis, "The dog is doing your stuff and will die if you don't figure it out."

My stuff? I am responsible? Where do I even start? Phil!

Phil's answer, "Look to your judgments"

A week went by with me meditating trying to figure it out. I cried daily over the probable death of my dog as he continued to decline. What could I be doing that was so detrimental to Rebel that it was destroying him? And then, in one blinding insight, it came to me as I watched a news program. It reported on a group of half dead pit bull, fighting dogs who had been forced to fight for their lives. The conditions in which these animals lived was so filthy and deplorable it made me want to hurt the people responsible. I felt hate welling up in my heart and that's when I realized what I was doing.

There had been many such reports of late and I found the energy surrounding my judgments and condemnation of those who committed such atrocities so strong and hateful it was actually killing my dog. And Rebel, no doubt, through his unconditional love for me was willing to take on the mirror to save me the grief and illness.

With this new insight, I got down on the floor with Rebel, gathered him into my arms and prayed the most loving and fervent prayer I ever uttered to be relieved of my hate and judgments no matter what they were.

And with that, Rebel got up and ran down the hall, spun around and came back to joyously lick my face. I swear this is the absolute truth.

What better or safer way to know ourselves than through association with loved ones? Had I not finally understood that my husband's lack of emotional communication was a mirror of my own lack of self awareness? As I began a spiritual dialogue with myself and Higher Guidance I was able to shed feelings of inadequacies and discover my own self worth.

And I had released the heavy negative emotions of hate and judgment to save my much loved companion. So strong is the energy of love and forgiveness, it can heal instantly. Think what this can mean for the health and well being of ourselves and our loved ones.

Chapter Sixteen

Seven years flew by as my children grew into young adults and I began to form plans for a life of my own. I met a Connecticut Yankee through an unusual Phil-driven exercise and moved there to live with him. Both children were of an age to live where they chose. They decided to remain in town, close to family and friends and continue the life they had built growing up, knowing they were free to visit me in Connecticut whenever they desired.

My Yankee husband, Zach, and I lived an organic lifestyle on five manicured acres along a lazy tidal river that meandered through a salt marsh, down to Long Island Sound on the Connecticut shoreline. We had a half acre of vegetable garden and we fished and lobstered on the Sound. I loved my garden and was overjoyed to be able to communicate with the Nature Devas of the area. It was the ideal life for me.

And I became quite a fisherman. Zach taught me how to bait the lobster pots thereby anointing me the master baiter. I thought my mother would pass out when I announced my new job description!

Zach had hacked the five acres from an overgrown landscape along the small river. From the cherry hardwoods he salvaged, he had beautiful kitchen cabinets designed for the split level house he had built.

The half of the property that faced the street was planted with White Pines and Douglas Firs, Yews and Blue Spruce, staggered three deep for privacy. Interspersed with those lush trees were Azalea, Hydrangea, Weeping Cherry, Japanese Maple and other equally lovely flora, especially in Spring. Springtime in Connecticut is a thrilling event. There were many varied potential conversations with Nature just waiting to be explored and enjoyed.

As a born and bred Yankee, Zach's attitude toward life was very different from mine. He never stopped working, always had a project going. It was his aim to be totally self sufficient, which he did accomplish with a lot of attention to detail. He did not know from metaphysics but led an ethical life just because it was the right thing to do. His generosity was genuine and without strings.

I came along and showed him that work could become play and still be productive; a way of life that I espoused totally. When he caught me talking to the plants he asked to be remembered, saying, "Say hello for me," or, "What's the news from the squash today?" His sense of humor had no bounds, which was often put to the test as our family grew.

The biggest change I brought to Zach's life was a parade of animals that I introduced, one by one, to our household. After initial objections, Zach gave it up after he fell in love with each one in turn.

The first addition was the little fluffy French Lop eared bunny that later, amazingly, morphed into a 25 pounder. Shortly thereafter came Detroit, an orange marmalade kitten, who wrote letters home to my family and was Bunner Rabbit's playmate. Next came a blue eyed, blue merle Australian Shepherd puppy we named Matilda, who loved to wallow at the muddy edge of the river. On a trip back to Florida I adopted a pair of downy China goslings, O.J. and Skids, in a moment of insanity. These cuties imprinted on me and would not go into the water unless I got in there with them. There was Gwendolyn, the little Rouen duckling who loved to watch TV with us nestled on Zach's chest and who, sadly, became dinner for the local fox. And finally there was Rebel, the black tri-colored Aussie puppy, a roly-poly ball of fur gifted without any admonition from Zach to keep him off the bed. It was a loving and noisy family there on the five acres.

I should tell you how I met Zach. It's a funny story and one just dripping with metaphysical undertones.

As I have said, I grew up in the cotton growing Delta of Mississippi, along the mighty river. I used to ride my horse and deer hunt along the levy. I loved the country and the freedom I had as a child. Needless to say, city living is not my thing. For most of the years of my marriage to the children's father I tried to get the family to move to a less populated area. However, I was the only one who did not love city living in Fort Lauderdale.

After divorce and my decision to continue into a professional PhD program, I spent a couple of weeks every summer break touring New England. I had planned to move there and practice when the children were old enough to be on their own. Rhode Island and Vermont were my first choices. I had learned to alpine ski in Vermont and loved the country side and quaint colonial towns.

I would fly up to Albany, NY, rent a car and head across the Hudson River into the wilds of Vermont. Flying into Providence I would tour the rural areas of Rhode Island around the University. To me, Connecticut was just a long stretch of I-95, constipated with toll booths that made traffic a nightmare between New York and Rhode Island. It took a special person to introduce me to the beauty and history of the state.

I made many friends along the way; people with whom I am still in contact. One suggested I subscribe to a magazine called "MOTHER EARTH NEWS." Besides the excellent articles on country living there were classifieds in the back section advertising opportunities for employment, businesses for sale, real estate, farms, farm animals, etc for sale. It turned out to be an excellent suggestion.

I had been tracking a health food store for sale in Killington, VT through the classified section for months. Not that I wanted to actually own a health food store, but it was selling at a reasonable price, in a place I wanted to live, and I enjoyed fantasizing about it. When I talked to the children about it they just fell over laughing. They wanted to know why I had been knocking myself out for years in school and only to run a grocery store. I figured I could do counseling in the back office. Besides, I was getting mighty tired of writing research papers.

The day my August issue arrived I had been slaving over problems for sadistics; which should tell you how I experienced the subject of Statistics. Thrilled to have an excuse to take a break I grabbed the magazine and flopped on the sofa to check out the status of the health food store in Killington. The ad, previously at the front of the business section, had been moved to the last ad in the section, right above the Personals.

The first personals ad was a really long one. My thought, when my eye caught it, was that the writer must be pretty desperate to spend so much money placing an ad of that size. It was half a column long.

The ad's first line read in big bold print," FINANCIALLY INDEPENDENT AND SECURE, ATTRACTIVE 43 YEAR OLD MALE…" but before I could enjoy a good laugh, my heart started to pound, my mouth went dry, I broke a sweat and my eyes felt like they were shooting out of my head. Really! Remember those Tom and Jerry cartoons where Tom would see Jerry setting fire to Tom's tail or something equally outrageous, and his eyes would just pop out of his head? I swear, that is just how my eyes felt. A shot of adrenaline right in both eyes!

My reaction was a little unsettling, to say the least. After my heart slowed down and I got my eyes under control, I realized that I'd better pay attention to this ad and read it all the way through. The writer wanted "…a well educated, highly attractive female, between 38 and 45 who loves fishing and farming and wants to live an organic lifestyle…" The writer lived in Connecticut along Long Island Sound and had five acres and a 5 bedroom house to share.

This man is totally insane to write an ad like that, I thought. No telling how many desperate and lonely women with problems would answer it and not be truthful about their situation. Hadn't this man heard of Fatal Attraction?

I decided I should answer the ad. I had great fun writing about myself, several pages worth, and I was totally truthful. I included what I thought was an unflattering photo of myself in salt sprayed, old jeans standing on deck of a friend's boat and left the letter for the post person to pick up. Answering the ad was just a brief and enjoyable respite from the agony of sadistics. I really didn't expect an answer anyway.

The response from Connecticut arrived four days after I posted my letter. It might go on record as the fastest the US Postal Service ever acted. A large manila envelope arrived containing a very well written response and photos of a gorgeous man with blond curly hair and startling gray eyes. There was an aerial shot of his house surrounded by acres of yard on a small river and a three-quarter view of his thirty foot fishing boat. His photo showed him looking through the forward cabin window of the boat. I could not tell his height or if he was impaired in any way. I still could not believe that a man this attractive and apparently well off was advertising for females in a magazine. Something had to be terribly wrong with him.

Deciding to get crafty, my response asked several questions. Education? He was a Yale grad, with an MBA from Dartmouth (yikes!). Married? Divorced with 3 teenaged children living with their mother but close by. (ok). Did he like to dance? (figuring this would tell me if he was sound of body). He had built a discoteque in the basement of his home and took dancing lessons in the winters to stay in shape (OMG!); His height was 6' 4" and weight was 190. (Holy Moses!) He supplied his phone number and left it up to me to call if I felt comfortable doing so. Well!

Here was the perfect person for me, it seemed. But I was not looking for a relationship. Between school and work I really did not have time for one. But after my over the top physical reaction to the ad, I had to trust that something important was underway for me. I could have ignored the invitation to call. The choice was mine. Besides, the man was safely over a thousand miles away and I was terminally curious.

I decided to call. The first question out of my mouth was "Why did you feel the need to advertise for someone? You appear to have all the right stuff to attract a mate."

Zach responded, "I've had several short relationships since my divorce but I seem to wear the ladies out. They love the trappings of what I have to offer but don't want to do the work it takes to help run a self sustaining lifestyle. I want a partner who loves the work as well as the perks. My friends have told me I was crazy to advertise. I was beginning to think they might be right. You should read some of the weird letters I got along with some truly kinky photos."

Totally unsurprised there...

Our first conversation lasted over two hours. Zach was well spoken and courteous. He never pressured me in any way. He wanted to send me an airline ticket to visit when I was ready. So between August and Thanksgiving, there were many letters, photos and conversations exchanged. When we finally did get together we were old friends. Zach was a man who had no problem sharing thoughts or feelings, and, I am pleased to report, was verbally and physically affectionate.

I spent that first Thanksgiving weekend visiting him in Connecticut, nearly freezing to death. Zach had to pry me away from the wood stove he kept going for me; This thing was a huge metal structure built in place and could be fed in both the kitchen breakfast nook area as well as the living room. I called it the Crematorium. Just keeping the monster fed took a major outlay of planning and muscle. The 3,500 square foot house had central heat and air but Zach was determined to use the seven cords of wood he personally cut every year from a wooded property he owned and stacked in the wood shed. An occupation I later came to know and dread every spring.

Deciding to give Zack and his lifestyle a trial, I placed an ad to rent my house furnished before moving to Connecticut. I wanted to close out the term and pay off my student loan before I left.

A interesting lady about my age answered the rental ad pretty quickly. She arrived at the house after dark, wearing a head scarf and glasses with tinted lens. Though her appearance was initially off putting, after introductions, I found she had a lovely energy. I liked her and felt comfortable turning my house over to her.

She told me she had a ten year old son and the house would be perfect for them. Even though I asked for only the first and last month's rent she paid me for the whole year in cash! That certainly covered my loan with a little left to put in the bank.

Later in the summer I got a call from my sister, Cindy, telling me that she had gone by the house several times and there appeared to be no one living there. And according to the neighbors, no one had ever moved in. Cindy had monitored the mail just in case it was a drug drop but nothing untoward was going on. Strange, indeed.

After six months more of no activity, Cindy rerented the house to a couple of doctors relocating from the north.

Zach and I became totally involved with each other and the life we were building. It definitely was a mutual love match. We married the following year. We had four extraordinary years together before a heart attack took him away at age forty-seven. I have always said that his example was a great recommendation for living a life of unhealthy hell raising. Zach and I lived an exemplary organic existence, fishing and farming, and he died anyway; far too young.

He was a larger than life character. Friends spoke of him for years as if he were still alive. He loved his life and his friends. He loved dancing and a good party. He was there for all of us when we needed him. He instilled in me a great determination to continue to live simply and with respect and honor for the earth's great gifts.

Zach was there for me for almost two years after he died. I would often feel him touching my head to comfort me, particularly when I was sad or missing him. He popped in and out of my dreams, always smiling. And because I was willing to trust my Inner Guidance, Zach got me to the Northeast in a way I never would have imagined, offering a wonderful and loving relationship and lifestyle so dear to my heart.

Chapter Seventeen

A year after Zach left us I bought a small house a mile from the little town next door along the Sound. This beautiful little colonial town could have been plucked right out of a Currier and Ives print. There were antique houses dating from the 1700s that surrounded the town green; some still used as residences and a few converted to art galleries and boutique shops. Enormous Maple trees lined the paths through the Green. Rebel and I loved making the Green our last walk before bed.

After selling the house and five acres, I found homes for the geese on a farm in Rhode Island. Bunner Rabbit became a pet with friends on Block Island, RI. Matilda became a mommy in upstate Connecticut and stayed as a brood bitch for an Australian Shepherd show kennel there. I visited all of them from time to time.

Rebel, Detroit and I moved to the funky little house on three quarters of an acre on the edge of town. The house was situated next door to fourteen vacant acres and across the street from a thousand acres of wooded preserve. Ours was one of four houses that spun off a short driveway from the main road and ended at a large salt marsh on a tidal river that flowed into the Sound. These salt marshes and tidal rivers make up most of the Connecticut shoreline.

The first time I saw the house was a couple of years earlier. Zach and I had gotten lost trying to find the Nature Conservancy Preserve's trail head to do some hiking with the dogs. When we realized we were right across the street from the entrance, we pulled into a driveway to turn around. There, I saw a small house perched on a glacial erratic (a sheer rocky outcropping) of over 6 feet above the lower lawn. Two apple trees flanked the driveway and a full sized, antique farm wagon rested on the fore point of the rocky rise.

What had caught my eye was the profusion of bright orange Nasturtiums spilling out of the wagon, trailing along its rustic sides. It was a charming sight and one I thought I might try to duplicate back at the house with a big terra cotta pot. I thought of that house often over the ensuing two years. So you could say that Zach found that little house for me. I bought the house with the condition that the wagon would remain. I filled it with Nasturtiums every year.

Rebel and I walked the Nature Conservancy's woods almost every morning. In fact we were frequently lost in them. It was easy to get off trail as I often walked with my head down looking for interesting flora or up for the many species of birds and creatures that inhabited the woods. Rebel loved to take off chasing small furry creatures. The ethereal beauty and peaceful energy of the woods was an excellent place to do a walking meditation.

As a herding dog, Rebel wasn't the best help in finding the way back to the trail. After being lost for over two hours in the woods one summer afternoon it became clear to me that I really had no idea just how large a thousand acres actually is.

When Rebel flopped down in from of me, panting, I figured it was time to ask Phil if they could help us find our way home.

Since the woods had put me in an altered state from the beginning of the trail, all I had to do was stop moving, get centered and ask. Instead of getting the usual response from Phil I began to feel a gentle vibration, rather like a mild tickling sensation playing along my body. This wasn't Phil. It was an energy, playful and teasing. I wondered if this might be a wood sprite or one of the flora devas. It seemed to have a direction so I decided to follow it. Whatever it was, the playful energy made me giddy and reluctant to leave the woods.

"Let's just stay and play for a while," I said to Rebel.

Rebel would have none of it and started a deafening barking campaign that let me know his sentiments in no uncertain terms.

I felt it was prudent to decline the invitation to play and thanked the spirit for its help. "It's time to go home."

That's when I heard the sounds of conversation nearby. Realizing that this must be a residence that backed on the woods, I headed in that direction. But in order to reach the house Rebel and I had to climb a steep hill. I was often on my hands and knees, grabbing for small brush, to keep from sliding back down the incline.

When Rebel and I threw ourselves onto the yard, we found two young mothers enjoying each other's company while watching their young ones at play. I apologized profusely feeling totally foolish.

"I'm so sorry to intrude but we're new in the area and totally lost. What street is this?" I asked, hoping that we were not too far from home.

Both women laughed and one said, "It is not unusual for us to find lost hikers in the back yard. If you had walked just a little further on you would have found the slope not nearly as steep. Take a moment to rest and, if you need, one of us can drive you to your car."

"I hope I'm not that far from home since we entered the woods at the trail's head across the street from my house. I'm sure we can walk home if you point us in the right direction."

As it turned out we were clear on the other side of the woods and did need a ride. I sincerely hoped to meet any future neighbors in a less strenuous way.

After that, I noticed that Rebel had taken up a practice that I found both amusing and dear. When it became clear to him that I was wandering aimlessly, he would follow, bumping me with his nose and then running back to the path. He would do this several times until I either got the message or we got too far from the trail. At that point he would just drop down in front of me and lie there until I took notice of him or fell over him. He may not have had the nose of a hound but he had the smarts of the herding breeds.

I did not meet the wood spirit again, I'm sorry to say, but there were many other interesting energies present there. The woods wake up in the spring and produce the most amazing flora. The beautiful colors and fragrant odors can make you light headed. Standing quietly, all alone, eyes feasting, ears listening to the murmur of the trees, I would say is a peak experience, a true oneness with All That Is.

No where was this brought home to me than the morning I happened upon a small clearing where a soft ray of sunlight was beaming down on a single wild purple and green striped Jack in the Pulpit flower. The little thing stood firmly rooted, bathed in the sun, with its leaves reaching upward. I *knew* it was giving thanks to its creator for the opportunity to express life. I don't know how long I stood there, tears streaming down my cheeks, so grateful to share a very special moment.

Rebel turned out to be quite a provider for us, though I did not understand the need for such a service. I found him one morning on the back deck guarding a small brown paper bag folded neatly at the top. He relinquished the sack happily, wagging his whole body, since Aussies are born without prominent tails. Opening the sack I discovered that he had brought home a half dozen assorted fresh bagels. He did this on several occasions until I realized the small bakery at the end of our road was the source. I shopped there frequently, never realizing my dog was panhandling at the back door.

I had a funny image of the baker saying, "That black dog is here again. Give him the day olds."

I never did discover where Rebel snatched the perfectly grilled, whole chicken breasts he brought home. There were three in all, on three separate occasions. He had soft mouthed them all the way home, as there was hardly a tooth mark on them. I suspect that one of my neighbors decided it was prudent to have someone guard the family grill after mysteriously losing three of his carefully prepared, anticipated dinners.

As a matchmaker, however, Rebel fell way short of the mark.

Strolling through the town green one sunny spring day with Rebel on leash, I was yanked out of my reverie (I really don't spend all my time with my head in the clouds, though that is when the most interesting and extraordinary things happen to me) by Rebel's dash to say hello to a nice looking, well dressed man sitting quietly on a bench. Rebel was all over the man as if he were an old friend.

I had quite a job pulling Rebel off the guy. He was practically crawling into the man's lap.

"I'm so sorry. I don't know what got into him. He is usually a well mannered dog," I explained to him.

"No apology necessary. I have never understood why, but animals seem to love me. Your dog's behavior is nothing new. My names is Drew. Who is this gorgeous creature?" he asked, giving Rebel a good scratch behind his ears.

I introduced myself and Rebel. We chatted with Drew for a minute and then I dragged my dog off to continue our walk. Further down the path I said to Rebel and Phil, "Interesting Guy. Interesting to note a little leap of my heart rate. Hummm..." Not a word from either one.

Chapter Eighteen

When a call came from my neighbor excitedly asking me to come over I prayed that Rebel had not rolled in her flowerbed again. Rebel and his best bud, a black Lab named Jones, chased geese on the salt marsh almost every morning, coming home covered in marsh muck and God only knows what else. Since I chased him out of my garden he often availed himself of our neighbor's. I frequently and surreptitiously replaced small plants to cover his sins.

Arriving at her front door she was all smiles (whew!) and invited me back to the laundry room. Her three children were gazing transfixed into a laundry cart where nestled a litter of newborn kittens being lovingly cared for by their mom.

"They were born over night. We didn't know she was pregnant. We actually didn't know she was a she! The kids found her and brought her home a few weeks ago."

With a sincere plea she said "Please, please adopt one. I cannot bare to take them to the shelter and there are so many of them! I know you just lost Detroit. And most of these are orange marmalades."

I had, in fact, lost my beautiful Detroit to the street right at the end of our shared driveway. It happened in an odd way. I drove home one evening and saw Detroit's lifeless body on the road just as I was about to turn into the driveway. I stopped the car and ran to the spot where I saw him. He had been hit by a vehicle and left in a pool of blood. Tears spilling down my face, I put the car away and went to the house to grab something to wrap my cat in for burial. I was on my way back out, and full into mourning his death, when I encountered Detroit just waking up from a nap in the kitchen bay window. He stretched and strolled over to wind himself all around my legs in greeting.

"Detroit! You're not dead! Then what is that out on the street?" I picked him up for a big hug and left to see what cat was dead at the end of the drive.

I was flabergasted to find there was nothing there. No cat, no blood. Nothing.

Totally perplexed I rushed back into the house to make sure Detroit was still there.

"Well, you little rascal. Are you playing games or am I just bananas? OK, the jury is still out on that." I was left to ponder that whole episode for days.

Exactly one week later I found Detroit dead, in a pool of blood at the end of the shared driveway. He had given me a week to get used to the idea that he was ready to pass on.

So, returning to my neighbor's plea, I agreed to take one of the kittens; and ended up with three! All of us who agreed to take kittens handled them every day so they would be easy to hold and love. Cats can be notoriously snotty when it comes to being cuddled. So we wanted these kittens to think we were part of their litter by smelling our scent before they opened their eyes.

I took mine home when they were 6 weeks old and named them Grover and Smith and Wesson. Wesson never seemed at home with us and was adopted by the daughter of a friend. Grover and Smith, who became Smitty the kitty, fought over who would sit in my lap on lie on my chest. The loser had to take to the floor and cuddle up to Rebel.

Both turned out to be excellent cats. Mom cat got fixed as soon as possible and Grover and Smitty, being males, were neutered as well. One pair of fertile cats can foster a dynasty in short order.

Of the two, Smitty was the most loving and attached to me. His favorite past time was chasing me up the stairs at bed time and settling on my chest to sleep. It always tickled me to hear him running up the stairs because he was not one of those light-on- his feet cats. Where Grover was silent in his travels, Smitty made audible thumps when he moved around.

Smitty proved just how attached he was when he astral traveled to me while I was visiting friends in Uddevalla, Sweden. My last night there I was just cozying into the bed when I heard something run across the floor of my room. Since my friends had no pets my first thought was rats! Knowing that my hostess was too fastidious for that I sat up in the bed to see what had come into the room.

It was too dark for me to see what was running around on the floor. Just as I turned on the light the creature jumped on the bed and crawled into my lap. I could feel the weight of it but I could not see anything there. That was a little startling, to say the least. Something was in my lap that had no physical form!

My first impulse was to jump off the bed but then the creature began to purr and I experienced a moment of familiarity. Smitty! It just "felt" like him. He wasn't visible but he was tangible as a soft ball of energy. Thoroughly stunned, I laid back down stroking Smitty's astral form and talking softly to him. With that he moved to my chest, settled on my neck and then disappeared.

When I returned home the person who had been taking care of the house and animals was sorry to tell me that Smitty had gone missing a few days previously. She had searched but had not found him.

Later that evening as I was reading in bed before turning off the light, I heard something run up the stairs and across the floor. Thinking it was Grover I kept on reading until I felt him jump on the bed. I lowered my book to greet Grover but there was nothing on the bed. *Humm...that's interesting.*

"Smitty, is that you? " I felt him get into my lap and I went back to my book. Smitty stayed around the house for as long I lived there. I often wonder if the new owners inherited a ghost cat when they moved in.

I allowed all of my animals the freedom of the neighborhood in spite of losing Detroit and Smitty. I took each cat in turn, and sat with him in meditation, just as I had done with Rebel. With Phil's help I asked each cat's Spirit to keep him safe so that he might have the freedom of life a cat should have. I had to release each to choose his own way; either life or death. It was not an easy thing to do and only after a lecture from Phil that there is no death, neither human nor animal. Both my husband and Smitty had done a loving job of proving that to me.

Chapter Nineteen

At my small property I had managed to put in a decent vegetable garden and landscaped more flower beds than my yard could really handle. Everything was running smoothly and I realized I needed a new project. I love being creative but I had done myself proud on my home and gardens. There was no room for further creative effort at that time.

I'll just ask Phil their thoughts on the matter.

Several days of asking later I was looking through a high gloss, expensively published magazine advertising real estate properties. "Unique Homes Magazine" was the forerunner of Realtor.com. I loved to look through it and dream of owning a farm where I could have all the animals I found appealing - horses, dogs, cats, goats, chickens, geese, sheep, llamas...the list would be endless. Old MacDonald had nothing on my aspirations.

Turning to the section on Connecticut properties my eyes fell on a farm being advertised in the north western part of the state. And once again, as it had when I saw Zach's ad in "Mother Earth News", my whole body reacted to what was on that page. It was a farm of a hundred and fifty plus acres in Litchfield County. The house wasn't much to look at, being an old colonial, but the center isle horse barn was glorious. Instantly my mind was filled with images of what I would do living there.

I got up from my chair and ran to the phone to call the realtor advertising the property and made an appointment for the next day, and then tried to contain my impatience enough to wait for the time to go.

When I arrived at the farm the following day, I was disappointed to find that the place was rather run down and not at all what I expected. Someone had taken some very misleading photographs. However, the land was beautiful, even if the place would be a major project. Why had Phil gotten me all excited about this place?

The realtor showed me around, talking up the better points of the property, doing her best with a hard sell. While we were exploring an ancient out building her mobile phone rang out so loudly it startled the pigeons roosting in the rafters of the dilapidated old structure. She walked away, listening intently and then speaking softly.

Ending the call she looked at me thoughtfully and said, "That call was to tell me that we just received a new listing here in Litchfield County, about 15 minutes away. It's a pricey property, an old farm, totally renovated as a high end spa resort. It might be bought for a favorable price since it's looking for a quick sale. It has over a hundred acres with a ten acre lake. I don't have the final price as yet. Would you like to see it? You can follow me there and we can both take a look at it with the rest of my sales associates."

"Why not. I can tell you that this property would be way too much for me to undertake. I just finished a major reno on my present home and I am so over living with contractors and construction. But if this place is set up to run as a spa I would have no experience to take it on."

"It doesn't have to be run as a spa. You could run it as a fancy horse farm. Let's go see it. It might be fun for you. I have to go view it anyway."

As we hopped into our respective vehicles and sped away to check out the new property, I was beginning to feel a little excitement building in my chest. *What if... well don't get too excited. Just enjoy the day* I told myself.

Turning through a pair of bricked entry posts that flanked the driveway I saw a decorative sign announcing the name, Windy Hill. I followed the realtor up the long, tree lined drive. At the end it became a circular driveway that deposited us in front of a stately, white brick manor house built in the style popular during the American Federal period. It's broad front was unadorned except for the black shutters that outlined its many tall windows. There were four chimneys, one at either end of the two story center section of the house and one at either end of the two, one story wings. The house sat on an elevated area of the expansive lawn with lovely slate steps and walkway leading to the front door. I fell in love with it instantly.

This was my actual destination all along, I thought. *I just had to take a side trip to get here. But a spa?*

There were several ladies from the real estate office waiting for us. The owner of the property was also there. A slim and fit, very attractive lady in maybe her mid fifties. She introduced herself and offered to show us around. She was obviously proud of what she had created, and rightfully so. The grounds and landscaping were beautiful.

Walking into the spacious, two story foyer I felt like someone had kicked me in the chest. I took a deep breath and exhaled slowly. The interior was stunning, with highly polished antiques of the period. Lovely rich and colorful fabrics upholstered the furniture. We were shown through one gorgeous room after another. Each of the eight bedrooms with en suite and owner's apartment had a different color and theme. The place absolutely stole my breath.

I just kept questioning Phil, *"Are you insane? What am I supposed to do with a house this large? I don't know how to run a spa, even if I wanted to. And never mind what the dogs and cats would do to all this beautiful furniture."* In their usual manner, not a word...

The tour continued on past a huge indoor swimming pool with suites of exercise and massage rooms down one side. We exited the house to tour the formal gardens, across a broad green lawn and strolled down to a sparkling ten acre lake with its white Victorian gazebo gracing the end of the dock. I stood there looking out over the lake, my eyes taking in its serenity and the beauty of the fall foliage. It was a magnificent property. I just could not imagine what I was to do with it and especially how I was to afford its four million dollar price tag. What was Phil thinking?

Turning my attention back to the owner I realized she was speaking to me. ",,,and there is also a large horse barn that needs very little renovation. We have walking and riding trails to accommodate horses if you wanted to add riding to the programs I have suggested."

"Horses?" My body began to tingle. Maybe I should pay better attention.

She took my hand and said, "Walk with me."

She led me to a path that meandered around the lake. "I have just found out that my husband is terminally ill. I must devote all my attention to him. I would love to have someone appreciate what I have put in place here. It is all ready to go. You just have to push the button.

"I already have reservations starting in the spring. I have a staff hired, ready to go to work. There is a farm manager's house at the far end of the property. There are two high end magazines and the New York Times ready to interview me and make the announcement of our grand opening in April. The possibilities are enormous for making this place pay for itself and possibly make a profit by its second year. Please give it some serious thought. I can tell you love the place."

"I'm absolutely overwhelmed by it, " I told her. "I can certainly see the possibilities. But actually finding a way to pay for it is another matter. I will have to consult my banker and let you know."

Walking back to the house ideas flooded my brain. I began to see how I could grow the food for the spa. God knows I am an excellent farmer if nothing else. And there is a farm manager. We could hay the fields for sale as well as to feed the horses. I could rent stalls and have a day riding program for locals. The spa itself would produce revenue on a daily and weekly schedule. I could actually do counseling.

I said goodbye to all and promised I would get back to them within 24 hours. On the drive home I felt an energy build in my solar plexus until I thought I would explode.

Without an appointment I stopped by my bank and asked to speak to the person who helps me with finances. As I began to speak about the spa exhilarating words come out of my mouth that I had not anticipated. I began to outline a program for the property. My banker showed interest in my sales pitch and called in two loan officers.

Once again words poured forth. The energy coming out of my mouth was so strong I could have bitten the heads off nails. Where was this coming from? By the time I was through, the loan officers had agreed to lend me the whole four million dollars with the spa as collateral.

I left the bank in a daze. As the adrenalin began to subside I began to question what had just transpired. What had I set in motion?

"Oh. My. God! I could be four million dollars in debt!"

I called the bank when I got home and told them I would give them an answer regarding the loan in a couple of days. Then called the realtor and told her I needed a couple of days to think. She told me not to take long as it was a hot property. Did I want to tie it up with an option? I told her that I could not do that right at this time.

And then I got on a plane and flew to Florida to visit family and to think things over. I just could not make that big a decision without some careful consideration, no matter how strong the energy or what Phil had to say about it.

After four days in Florida driving myself bonkers, I decided to go ahead with the spa. There were just too many ways to make that place pay for itself. My banker said the property alone would appraise at over four million even with no business attached.

And there was the fact that it came through Higher Guidance, Phil, whose wisdom steered me in a direction that was basically well thought out. What money was needed, the bank was willing to lend. And the property came with a way to pay for itself. What more could I ask? With Source and Phil behind me I could not fail. The synchronicity and energy were just amazing.

Returning home I called the realtor first to tell her my decision. She was very sorry to tell me that while I was gone, a large corporation made a cash offer for Windy Hill and it was accepted. They had tried but no one knew how to contact me.

Hadn't she warned me to lock the sale in with an option but I was too afraid to commit myself to the project on site. Major disappointment settled in and I was left wondering what happened.

"What did I do wrong?" I asked Phil.

"You did nothing wrong. Even though everything was all laid out for you, you were just not ready to take immediate action on an opportunity of this scale. You always have the right to choose. That is what life is, a series of decisions and choices that determines personal creativity. But you have to admit that the Creative Principle, responding to your very powerful desire, presented you with an elegant example of the Law of Attraction in action.

"Everything has a timing," Phil continued. "Why do you think the energy was so unusually potent for this project? You could have acted on it immediately and trusted the outcome. Living consciously requires trust. You have lived with us in your heart and consciousness for many years now not to know the difference between beneficial, conscious action and something that is just a good idea.

"A good idea can present itself with interest or fun and may be beneficial. But conscious creation comes with a tiger on its tail. It's unmistakable. You felt that tiger in the bank while you were convincing the loan officers to make you a loan of four million dollars.

"We know you are disappointed but you will recover. Any action or decision, whether advantageous or not, is always a personal choice. There will be others."

"Yeah," I replied half heartedly. " But not as spectacular as this one. Can't you fix it?"

"This creativity is between you and the Creative Principle, as we prefer to describe the creative aspect of Source. We are no more powerful than you. Our job is to alert and advise, to guide. Remember, we are One. We, Phil, are the nonphysical aspect of Us. We have a greater or different perspective but that is all. You, our physical aspect, have free will, choice, and the ability to act upon your options. That is the gift of a physical experience. It is a special gift to Our Self as we live the physical experience through you. Excitement for All."

At least one positive thing to come from the experience in that it started me thinking about actually buying a farm - a small one - where I could toil away in my gardens and play with the animals. I put that to the back of my mind and settled back into my quiet life on my little piece of land.

Chapter Twenty

I want to share another story about trusting Higher Guidance. Making a clear intent for anything; a change for a better life, a new job, a romance, a new car, whatever you want, can be attained if you just put it "out there." Source, through your Higher Guidance, will get you where you want to go if you trust the process.

This is a story I was told by a lady who read my Tarot cards in Talkeetna, Alaska, at the annual Moose Droppings Festival.(yep, your heard it right).

Two years after Zach's death, I had been knocking around Alaska on a three month spiritual quest, camping by myself, glacial river rafting, hiking, and howling with the wolves. That whole trip is another amazing story in itself, but for now, I want to share an interesting side story of that trip.

I had come out of the Alaskan bush after a couple of weeks alone. I was dirty, sweaty, looking like hell and in bad need of a bath and human kind. The festival was lively enough to catch my eye as I drove past and figuring it would just fit the bill, I made a U turn and went to join the fun.

Walking around enjoying a huge warm pretzel dripping with mustard, I looked down an open lane of booths and was captivated by the eyes a woman seated on a platform behind a table with her bandaged leg propped up on a chair. There was a big sign overhead that read TAROT READINGS $5.

Ah, this should be fun, I thought. I would have strolled on over to her even if I had not felt summoned by her energy.

Her invitation was irresistible. Her eyes were even more compelling the closer I got. She looked to be around thirty five, a little on the plump side, good skin. Her sandy colored hair twisted a little messily on top of her head and the very colorful prairie skirt draped over her bandaged leg told me she was at ease with herself and her environment. She was attractive in an odd and interesting way. She offered her hand, and, in taking it, I felt a strong exchange of energy between us.

"Sit," she commanded, indicating the wooden chair opposite the table. "You're here because of two men, one you've lost and one you've given up for lost."

Tears immediately started spilling out of my eyes. Some emotion I was unwilling to name was vying for my attention.

She gave me a moment and then said,. "We are alike. We trust the Heavens to give us grace and guidance. Yet you are filled with sadness."

She patted my hands and continued, "You are going to be fine and do good works. Just give yourself time to fully forgive yourself for not being able to save him and understand that your husband's death was his own program."

How could she know about my guilt around my husband's heart attack? A loaded gun in his back could not have gotten Zach to go to the doctor in time. No matter what I advised he did not make an appointment until a week before he died. Yet…

"As to the second man who was instrumental in bringing you to Alaska, this is a good time to reconsider what you really want to do with your life. You know this man has issues to resolve and you cannot save him from himself either."

"It's true," I told her. "I just realized on the drive up through British Columbia that this man has a serious drinking problem. I could not fathom why he kept starting ridiculous arguments. I finally understood that it gave him a reason to put several whiskeys under his belt to 'ease out.' He actually tried to blame me for his drinking.

"I have not spend a lot of time with this man prior to this trip. He travels a lot internationally but has a residence here in Alaska as well as in Connecticut. My dog is absolutely over the moon crazy about Drew. That's how we met. I was walking my dog in the park when Rebel dragged me over to drool all over the man. I have to admit, the man has a lot of animal magnetism. As a trained therapist. I cannot believe I did not see his drinking problem sooner."

"You weren't paying attention," whispered in my ear.

"One afternoon, just prior to taking the car ferry over to Alaska, I had had enough. I left him drunk on the floor in a cabin in the Yukon Territory. Dragging my bag down a dirt road in Dawson City, sniveling and cussing a blue streak, I wondered how I was going to get myself home.

"It took me three days to find a way out of Dawson City, and it would have taken longer if I had decided to go back to Connecticut. Apparently no one is ever in a hurry to leave the Yukon. I decided not to go home and flew into Alaska in an old DC 3. That decision has made for a magical adventure."

Wiping my eyes, I started to laugh, "It's funny when you think about it. I have no idea where my companion is now. But here I am."

She patted my hand again in her soothing way and said, "You'll figure it out. You already know what to do."

She looked into my eyes for a long moment and cocked her head slightly to the side as if she had made a decision, "You are a story teller so I will share my story for you to pass along." She had not even offered the Tarot reading yet. One hand was just resting on the cards and the other on my hand.

She started, "I had been waitressing in Fort Lauderdale for several years, having a grand time being young and partying to the extreme. It was the late 70s and we were all doing way too much drug experimentation.

"I had a wide circle of friends, none of whom had any ambition but to carry on the perpetual party. It was a familiar scene along the beach. One particular night I had done a little too much and found myself being dragged out of a swimming pool. Apparently I had fallen in and bumped my head.

"During my time in the pool I had a vivid dream that a wizened brown man, bundled in a heavy sheepskin coat was calling me. I could clearly see the very green, treeless hill he was standing on, beckoning me to come. He was ancient but I found him attractive in some weird way.

"Anyway, I knew it was time for me to quit the drugs before I damaged my mind and body. I had been secretly dreaming of a home and family for some time. A woman's body tells her when it is time to reproduce. But I intuitively knew I wouldn't find that dream in Fort

Lauderdale. So I made a pact with myself that I would leave South Florida and find a new life. I did not know where I was going or even what I was going to do when I got there. How I could afford such an adventure was a mystery as I had no education beyond two years of community college. I was 23 years old, fairly attractive and willing to work my way. I could carry a tray full of drinks with the best of them. My parents were not happy with my decision but made me promise I would stay in touch every week.

"My first stop was Orlando, thinking maybe Disney would be fun. That did not happen but I secured a good job at an upscale restaurant. One thing from the very beginning was clear and upper most in my mind. I wanted to be a good example for clean living. I found I loved children and naturally gravitated to them either at work or not. I stayed in a town until the urging to leave was too strong to ignore and somehow found the next place without any real effort on my part. The dream of that little brown man never left me. It had been so real.

"In Missouri I met my first spiritual person who introduced me to the Tarot cards and taught me how to read them. She was a regular at one of the restaurants where I worked and we often talked about trusting our chosen paths. At first I did not even know what a path was. I just knew she was a loving person who genuinely cared about people. This was when I really started longing for a home and children to love.

"She told me that my dream had great importance for me and I would one day understand it. When it was time for me to move on, she gave me her much loved Tarot deck and told me it would serve me well. I retired that deck years ago and use it only occasionally for myself.

"It took me three years following my impulses from Fort Lauderdale, across the country. One day I found myself in Anchorage, Alaska and realized I had nowhere else to go. I had not found my path; hadn't found a husband, hadn't even a clue what to do but continue to wait tables and give Tarot readings.

"I liked living in Alaska. I love it now. You've probably found the people here amazing and very open and friendly. Hardly anyone is from here, much like South Florida. I made many friends who were committed to healthy living, hiking, river rafting, skiing. We would often pack a lunch and head out to explore one of the national parks.

"It was a beautiful, sunny and crisp mid September day. I had been in Alaska for a year. My friends and I were hiking up a big green, treeless hill at Hatcher's Pass when I saw a little brown man wearing a heavy sheepskin coat come running over the hill top shouting and waving his arms. I couldn't believe it! Here was my dream in action.

Not wanting to get waylaid by what looked like a local tour guide my friends said they'd catch up with me later and they took off, leaving me to face the strange little man running towards me.

'Where have you been? Show me your hands,' the little man demanded as he reached me. Amused and curious, I put my hands out. He grabbed both of them, palms up and stared at them as if the key to life was written there. And perhaps for him it was.

"'You're it!' He exclaimed. 'I've waited ages for you. You took so long to get here. Didn't you get my message? I am the shaman of this area. But I am old and can't take these harsh winters any longer. I want to retire to Hawaii. You will be my replacement.'

"I personally thought the little man was crazy. What message? He had showed up in my dream, yes, but there was no message. I had no intention of being his replacement. I knew nothing about spiritual matters, especially Native Alaskan ones. I told him so in no uncertain terms.

"He brushed aside my objections as if they had no validity. 'I will teach you. You will learn. Get you things and move here.'

"I laughed. I can't move here.

"Here was the middle of nowhere. There was not a house, a tree, even a hut in sight. 'How would I support myself?' I asked him.

"'I have a gold mine,' he explained, 'it doesn't make a lot of money but it will support you better than your present circumstances.'

"How did he know my circumstances?

"I could not seem to get this person to listen to reason. I knew nothing of shamanism and certainly did not want to work a gold mine. But he was so happily planning my future and envisioning his in Hawaii that his ears were deaf to my objections.

"Finally he grabbed my hand and proceeded to pull me up the hill. I am not a small woman as you can see. But this little man had a grip like a line backer and fairly yanked me up and over the hill toward an old Jeep parked below.

"There was a man standing beside the Jeep, a darn good looking man, strong and tall, a mess of red hair, looked to be about thirty years old. He had a grin on his face that bespoke a good sense of humor. I like him immediately. Maybe he could talk some sense into the shaman.

"'This is my foreman who oversees the gold mine. He's single and in need of a wife.' With that the little man placed my hand in the foreman's hand and danced a little jig, no doubt with visions of warm weather and swaying palms.

"The rest is history, as they say. We've been happily married for ten years and have four wild and wonderful children. The gold mine continues to produce a good living and I am now in charge of the spiritual community here in this area."

What a story! I know I got the short version. But the essence of Spiritual Guidance was front and center. I love to hear this kind of life experience. Especially when the person living it is consciously aware that there is more to physical existence than evidenced by our five senses.

She did eventually read my cards and told me some things I needed to hear, but mostly what I did not want to hear; that I was destined to be a solitary person because I was so comfortable and occupied with my non-physical teachers as well as the loving, four legged creatures I brought into my life. I would always live an extraordinary spiritual life while being physically focused.

I thanked her and walked away with much to think about. Could I have a relationship and continue to explore the non-physical? It was my choice. Life is always a choice, sometimes not always an easy or happy one.

Though I did worry about Drew, he made it home safely to Connecticut. We had one further strange encounter. I made an evening appointment to meet at his house up on the Connecticut River to pick up a couple of things I had left there. The minute I walked in the door I got a headache and felt light headed. As I hastily got my things together Drew followed me apologizing and trying to make amends.

I finally said, "Look, my head hurts and I just can't think about us at this minute. I have to get home."

Drew gently took my arm, "I can see you're not feeling up to snuff. Let me give you a massage for your headache. It'll make you feel better for the ride home. And we can talk."

"Thanks, but maybe some other time." I had to get out of there.

The drive home was a forty minute trip making it quite late when I got into bed to meditate. My head was pounding and I really was feeling weird. It took a while to relax into a meditative state.

Just as I was beginning to feel a little better an astral form stepped out of the far corner of my bedroom and drifted towards me. I had the sense it was a male form. I could sense it rather than actually see it, but it was undoubtedly there. I did not feel threatened by it, but I was uncomfortable with the thing in my room and wondered why it was there. I was determined that it was not going to get near me.

The entity had a strong intent. It communicated clearly that it wanted to unite with me. There was no way I was going to allow for that. And what an expression...unite with? What did that actually mean? At this point I called for the entity to go away, leave my home. And when it did not respond I became apprehensive.

My first reaction was to get out of bed and run but I could not move. My physical body was relaxed and spread out in its back. As that thing continued towards me I realized I had to resist it in my astral body. I had no idea if I could even achieve this but my intent to resist must have been powerful. I came out of my physical body in fighting stance, ready for whatever it took to vanquish that astral form, which, at this time, had begun to be actually visible.

Was this because I was in the astral now? It amazes me now to remember that even in the astral, my mind and consciousness were active and clear. I planned, I strategized how to take this thing down.

It tried several times to hug me, with amazing determination. I fought with all my astral energy, holding my arms out in front of me, palms up, to forestall any "uniting." After what seemed like a long time, I could feel myself wearing out. I was totally terrified at this point, knowing I did not have a lot of strength left to fight.

How it got behind me I don't know, but I felt the entity attach itself to my back. Somehow this did not seem like fair fighting to me and it made me really angry. With every last bit of angry energy I had and a great prayer on my lips, I reached over my shoulders with both hands, grabbed a hold of that thing and body slammed it so hard that I actually heard it hit the floor. Up to this point I don't remember hearing anything. I had been engaged in a silent energy fight.

I watched it pick itself up and I could sensed its disappointment. It moved off saying, "I only wanted to help you feel better."

I sprang up off the bed, now in full control of my physical body. "What was that thing?" I demanded of Phil as I ran around the house turning on lights.

"That was Drew. He meant you no harm. He really wanted to make you feel better."

"Never! Never! Never! How can I be sure this will never happen again?"

Phil's response was one of amusement, "You can always say that your are currently unavailable for uniting."

"Currently unavailable for uniting? Seriously?" I sat up for the rest of the night, refusing to sleep...just in case.

One further note on Drew. Some weeks later, after relating the experience to a friend, we decided to check the Akashic Records for information on him. What I got was this: "The file of the sorcerer is unavailable." Interesting...I never spoke with Drew again.

Chapter Twenty One

After Alaska, I was at loose ends for a while. Along with gardening I did a little writing but nothing that excited me. I finished a children's book I had started when my children were youngsters, and a memoir about the pair of geese, OJ and Skids, Zach and I raised. I was, however, journaling as I had daily sessions with Phil. This always brought me an excitement about the nonphysical world.

There were spiritual groups of various persuasions in the area. Many groups were sincere and many were just ego trippers, looking to exercise what they considered power over those poor souls willing to relinquish their own power. I found a couple of worthy groups I enjoyed and met some interesting and evolved people.

One group was led by Pat Rodagast who channeled Emanuel. I still have her book and Emanuel's wonderful and loving perspective. Pat has passed on but remains in our hearts through her great work with Emanuel.

During this time I was made aware of a group of people in Virginia doing research on the impact of sound on the hemispheres of the brain and altered states of consciousness. Because my initial awakening was through alpha sound impulses emitted by the brain I was interested to know the results of their research. And for whatever reason I have always been interested in sound.

Music was naturally my first interest and introduction to the effects of sound on the body. I studied ballet for many years and as a teen, fell in love with the music and rhythms of rock and roll. I dance my booty off whenever I get the chance.

The insistent drum beats of certain music can alter consciousness as well as heal disease, science has informed us. And many cultural religions have espoused drumming for healing and altered states. I still find this vastly interesting.

It started when I kept experiencing discomfort with a periodontal problem. My dentist said I would have to undergo some radical gum scraping to fix it. Never being a calm dental patient, I resolved to see if I could heal the problem myself with sound. I took the question to Phil.

"Hey, Guys, I could really use some help with my ailing gums. Can I heal them myself? I cannot face the pain of the dental solution."

"Try an A tuning fork," was Phil's answer.

I didn't know if there was such a thing as an A tuning fork but soon discovered I could purchase one at my local music store. Getting the thing home, I took it to my meditation chair and stared at it. I played around with it, hitting it on several surfaces and found it gave off the highest resonance when I hit it on a rock I had brought home from Alaska.

"Now what?" I asked aloud. Phil must have been out to lunch as there was nothing from the other side.

I decided to put the tuning fork right on my gums where I had the most pain. Every time I touched my gums, the vibration naturally ceased. So I next tried just holding it off the surface but found that tickled a little too much. Finally I held the fork on the outside of my mouth, as close to the skin as possible without touching it. I did this for about ten minutes until I got bored. I repeated the procedure before bed and a couple of times a day for about a month. The pain began to subside in a few days and gradually disappeared over the month.

I took the results to my dentist, who was amazed at what he saw, or rather did not see, in my mouth. He got so excited he called in his partner and both of them got into my mouth with their instruments and started speaking in dentistry.

It seems that dental research was being done with electrical impulses on types of periodontal problems and the tuning fork had replicated some of the results. Well...

There was another instance when sound came into play healing me. I had injured my right knee over-riding a spinning cycle. After three months my knee got a little better but I could not use it as I had before. It was painful to stand or walk for any length of time. And worst, it was keeping me from my gardens. I figured I'd have a bum knee the rest of my life. Not a happy thought for an active person.

My friend, Margo, who is a licensed massage therapist and as well as a professor of occupational therapy at a local university, told me come over. She offered to work on the knee to see if some physical therapy would help.

She put me on her massage table and started with a gentle knee manipulation. We weren't speaking while she was intent on what she was doing. As I was quite relaxed, allowing her to do her thing, an idea began to form in my mind. I asked her to put one hand on my knee and the other on the bottom of my foot.

"Let's make a sound. How about a strong AH? Don't try to sound good, just make the sound." I told her.

We tried a couple of uninspired sounds with nothing to show for them.

Determined, I asked Margo to muster any good energetic sound and let loose with it. At the same time I threw one out there to accompany it. At the moment the sounds came together I felt a strong energy blossom in my knee, shoot down my calf and out the bottom of my foot. It was so strong it brought me off the table. And it healed my knee instantly! There was no pain, no weakness and hasn't been from that moment.

Margo felt the energy in her hands but not as strongly as I did in my lower leg and the bottom of my foot. We were both amazed.

Needless to say the introduction to the research group in Virginia came through Phil in an amusing manner.

There is no place cozier on a snowy winter day than a bookstore. So, with the anticipation of curling up with a good read later in the afternoon, I took a stroll through my favorite purveyor of books. I didn't have a particular title or author in mind. I was just browsing and enjoying the delicious smell of coffee that wafted through the store, when I found a book on the floor in the self help/New Age aisle. Picking it up to return it to the shelf I noticed that the title was JOURNEYS OUT OF THE BODY by Robert Monroe. *Humm, Interesting title*, I thought as I placed the book back on the shelf.

A little later someone tapped me on the shoulder and said, "I saw this book on the floor and thought you may have dropped it."

Humm..it's the Monroe book.

Taking the book, I read the back cover to see if it was a subject I wanted to pursue. Mr. Monroe had written about his experiences with astral projection and consequently founded an institute of study in rural Virginia. This was not a subject that I found particularly interesting, particularly after my run in with Drew in the astral. God only knows what else is floating around "out there."

I stuffed the book back on the shelf and made sure it was secure. When I carried my selected items to the cashier, she quoted the price of my purchases and asked, "Did you want to include this Monroe book?" She held a copy of JOURNEYS OUT OF THE BODY.

Laughing, I told her to include the book with the rest of my purchases. Clearly here was a subject that needed my attention. Will I ever get over being surprised by Spirit at work in my life? It can be too funny when your Higher Self has an agenda. I would probably get around to reading the book, but not right away. I did not realize then that this was the same group in Virginia who was researching the effects of sound on the hemispheres of the brain.

A couple of months later my friend, Margo, asked if I had read the Monroe book on out of body experiences. "No, but it's on my list," I answered, perhaps a little intensely. Someone *really* wanted me to read that book

She had just finished it and found it very interesting. She reminded me that I had related a similar experience that happened to me while I was living in Southern California.

At that time I was twenty one years old and working as a flight attendant for one of the major airlines. I hadn't thought about that incident in years.

When my California experience out of body occurred I had been sitting on the deck of a beachfront restaurant in Malibu. The deck offered expansive views of the Pacific Ocean. It was late in the afternoon. The sun was close to the water's horizon and caused sparkling color to dance along the waves. I had a glass of wine, barely touched, in front of me and had drifted into a very relaxed and peaceful state of mind. My date at the table was droning on about something totally uninteresting and I had tuned him out to focus my attention on the lively effect of the sun on the ocean.

The water had refracted the sunlight into beautiful colors. Their sparkling effects had created little rainbows that gave the water a fanciful appearance of tiny sprites flitting along the surface. The playful scene so captured my appreciation that I felt drawn to become part of it. I wondered what it would feel like to immerse myself in the water, to bathe in it, to play and roll around in it. And quite suddenly I *was* bathing in it. I was right out there in the water, splashing the colors, feeling the cool, wet ripples of water tickle my skin. It filled my senses and I could actually smell and taste the ocean. But more than that, I became the ocean. I felt wet and salty, expansive, and ancient. The feeling of timelessness was all encompassing. It was an exhilarating experience. There was no thought, just an amazing feeling of being part of something vast and maternal, nourishing.

When I heard my name called, it startled me. I had a feeling of raising my eyes and looking up to see the restaurant in the distance. There was an instance of understanding that the two people seated at the table on the deck were myself and my date. I had a split second of confusion, then realized I was not in my body. I experienced a moment of fear that I might not be able to return to my body. Then instantly I was back, sitting at the table, totally stunned by what had just happened to me. I tried to explain the experience to my date but apparently didn't do a very good job of it. After he took me home I never heard from him again. Oh well…

Looking back, I suppose that amazing incident was the very beginning of my pursuit to understand consciousness. I didn't even know what to call it then or how to label the experience. I just knew it was very different from my usual way of living and thinking. The experience was so powerful that I knew it was not some imagined, alcohol induced hallucination. I had drunk only a little of the wine, after all.

And since then, years of study and experience had brought me to a communication with my Higher Guidance that I was comfortable with as acceptable and beneficial for my enjoyment of life.

Remembering that experience, it made sense for me to give some thought to reading Monroe's book. But several weeks passed after that and I still had not read it. I awoke one morning hearing Phil, "It's time to go to the Monroe Institute."

"No, I don't want to go. Besides, I haven't read the book yet." I stated firmly.

Next morning I heard again, "Time to go to Monroe."

"I'm not going. I. Am. Not. Going…forget it.." *Geez, what is this?*

Phil bugged me all day about calling and booking the workshop. So I finally agreed, just to shut them up, saying, "OK, here's the deal. I am only free to go in August. The funds to go must be provided and I want some reliable proof that this is not just me messing with my own mind."

I am a great one for making deals with Phil. If you take up this practice with your Higher Guidance I warn you to keep those deals. There can be consequences as they are taken as sacred contracts. It is, after all, a contract with one's Self.

I felt reasonably safe in making the deal. It was June and I knew from Margo that the Monroe always had a five month waiting list. As to the funds being provided to go, I was just giving Phil a hard time. But the thing about wanting proof was a sincere request I made often. Since much of my life was so "out there" I often questioned it.

I made the call the next morning and, as expected, was told that the August class was full, did I want to book for October? I did not.

I dusted my hands, feeling fairly virtuous, and smirked, "That's that. I tried." Not a word from Phil. I dismissed their request from my mind.

Two days later The Monroe Institute called and told me there had been a cancellation in the August workshop. Did I want the space? I had a good laugh and gave it up. I put it on my credit card and resigned myself to going. TMI sent me an affirmation to memorize and told me to read JOURNEYS OUT OF THE BODY.

There was no getting out of it. I read the book. I was enrolled in the Gateway workshop, the prerequisite for all other TMI programs.

I called Margo to tell her about the "deal" I made with the Guides and to see if she would consider trying for an August space with me. Since she had already booked her workshop for later in the year during her break from school we didn't make the Gateway together. However, we have experienced many Monroe workshops and visits together since then.

After reading Robert Monroe's book, I understood why I was encouraged to attend. So much more was going on there than just learning to control out of body experiences. The mission of the institute is to promote expanded states of consciousness through scientifically based research in sound. Some very impressive people associated with research in consciousness were and are associated with TMI.

If you want to know more about The Monroe Institute check out the website at www.monroeinstitute.org.

I decided to drive down to Virginia from my home in Connecticut. It was a long drive. However, trying to get there by bus, train or plane proved to be more time consuming than driving. I was ready for a road trip anyway and looking forward to experiencing the drive down the Shenandoah Valley. Virginia was calling, granting me a feeling of wonder-filled expectation.

It is interesting to note that this visit to Virginia was the reawakening of a promise I made myself some 15 years earlier. On a driving trip by myself through Virginia I had a peak experience of coming home. I had the radio cranked up, all the windows were down and I was singing along with John Denver, "Take me home country roads....almost heaven..." I was filled with a longing so strong and full of happiness I thought my heart would burst. I said out loud, "I'm going to live here one day."

The Monroe Institute is situated on eight hundred acres of some of the most beautiful land the Virginia Piedmont has to offer. It is snuggled up to the feet of the Blue Ridge Mountains, 30 miles southwest of Charlottesville, an area so steeped in our early American history, that folks talk about Thomas Jefferson as if he were still around. I suppose his spirit is.

A chalet style building houses the programs and resident accommodations. There is another building for sound research and offices. In the center of acres of open, green lawn is a six foot tall rose crystal surrounded by a labyrinth. The views alone would raise anyone's consciousness. There is a small vortex of energy that plays around out on the lawn. It is often strong enough to feel when you step into it.

My first trip to TMI was in its early days when there were only 11 student rooms and 2 bathrooms. Each room is designed with two sleeping units. The bathroom situation was cause for endless jokes, since we spent a lot of time standing in line waiting to use one. The programs are designed for maximum relaxation and thus a very relaxed bladder. We were cautioned to go before each session. Otherwise a full bladder could pull us back to waking consciousness. As the institute gained in popularity more rooms and bathrooms were added for which we are all grateful.

I made the trip in good order and managed to find the place even without a GPS. No small feat that! Even knowing where it is I can still get lost on those back roads.

I parked the car out front of the building, a short walk from my assigned room as it turned out. I had arrived late afternoon. The sun was still high in the August summer sky and quite warm. I made a mental note to move my car to a shady area after I got settled in my room and decided to leave the car's windows down to allow for a cooler interior until then.

After being greeted and shown to my room by a TMI associate, I took my bag inside and unpacked. I dropped my wallet and large set of keys in the side pocket of the bag, zipped it up and stowed it under the desk on my side of the room.

There were several members already there and more to come. Our first gathering would be dinner that evening. Until then we were free to explore those glorious grounds. We were to be a full workshop of 22 participants. Later I was told that my roommate had cancelled at the last minute and I would have the room to myself.

I checked out my accommodations, not really knowing what to expect. I had read about the Controlled Holistic Environmental Chamber, the CHEC unit. It is an interesting creation designed around a twin sized bed, wall enclosed on all sides with a small curtained entry. The interior is set up with headphones and electronics for the piped in Hemisync sounds we would use to alter our states of consciousness. It proved to be a very comfortable and cozy space for sleeping as well as our sessions with Hemisync.

On the desk next to my CHEC unit was a sheet of information, a pad of paper and a pen. The pen was an inexpensive disposable. For some reason my eyes fixated on the pen. I found it unacceptable; more than that, I did not like it. Silly, I know. I couldn't get pass the feeling of disdain for that pen. I absolutely could not imagine using that pen during the program. I had to have the pen in my car. No other one would do. A quick trip to my car would solve that problem with little effort. I wanted to move the car to a shady place anyway.

When I reached my car I was surprised to find the door locked. I didn't remember locking it. *Well, the window will do.* But trying the window almost broke my fingers as I tried to shove my hand though the closed glass. *Damn*! I remembered leaving the windows down so the interior wouldn't roast with the August sun cooking the asphalt parking lot. The car was locked and the windows up. *Hummm, I'll just go get the keys, move the car and bring my pen to the room.*

Back inside I dragged my bag from under the desk, unzipped the side pocket to retrieve the keys. They were not there. My wallet was there but no keys. Odd, I remembered clearly putting them in the side pocket with my wallet.

Why aren't they there? OK, look again.

I searched every nook and cranny of the bag, turned it upside down and shook it. No keys. I went through my purse, I felt around by the bed and all around the desk. I went through the room twice, shaking my head, knowing full well I put the keys in the bag. Why weren't they there?

"Where are my keys," I demanded of Phil? Not a word did I receive from the nonphysical side. "Are we playing another game?"

I made another trip to the car to see if the keys were somewhere around the area or maybe locked inside. I could see the pen I wanted but no keys. I looked all around the grass and up and down the walkway.

Back to the room and into my empty bag yet again. I turned it upside down and shook it again. There were no keys in it. I searched the room top to bottom, and went through the bag again. I took everything out of my purse and shook it upside down. No keys. By this time I was totally baffled and a little spooked. I was sitting on the floor with the bag in my lap, muttering to myself, apparently, since Phil was ignoring me, when a fellow attendee popped his head in the doorway.

"What's up, love? Need a hand with something?" he asked in his very Australian accent. "I'm Denis, I'm on my way home to Australia from Canada. Couldn't pass up the opportunity to experience Monroe since I was in the right hemisphere on business...pardon the pun."

"Hey Denis, I'm Claudia. I seem to have misplaced the keys to my car, even though I have a clear memory of putting them in the side pocket of my suitcase. I have gone through everything in this room several times. They are not here nor are they in my car. That set of keys is not a small item. There are house keys, office keys as well as car keys, all on a big purple clip. Hard to overlook, don't you think? They made a bulge in the bag."

"Surely they're here somewhere. We'll find them. Let's go look in the grass between here and the car. We'll get some of the others to help."

We found a few class members standing in the hall ready to walk down to the lake for a swim. They agreed to help look. We spread out in a straight line and walked slowly from the building to the car, a short walk across a small, well trimmed lawn and a flat asphalt driveway. No keys. I had not been anywhere else. I had been at the institute for less than an hour, most of which I had spent looking for the keys. Puzzling over the problem was giving me a headache and got me nowhere and no keys.

I gave it up and walked on down to the lake with the rest of the guys. The Institute is in a small valley through which the Rockfish River flows. Everything in August was full on green and fairly shimmering in the late afternoon sun. I just could not get enough of the vista.

We walked through pastures with cows and horses and fields of wild flowers. At the bottom of the walk was a small mountain lake. The perfect setting to separate one from the stress and cares of the day.

Our first assembly was at dinner that night where we all introduced ourselves and met our workshop facilitators. After dinner we gathered in a large, lushly carpeted room full of puffy pillows of various sizes and shapes. Here we were told to hand over all watches and any such timing devices. There were no small, personal cell phones at that time. For the duration of the workshop we would be centered in the present with no outside influences to dull our experiences. For the six days we were to be there, we would exist outside of time.

Maybe that was where I left my keys…somewhere in time, I mused.

Meeting everyone was a confirmation of the interest in the research being done at TMI. In this workshop there were people who came from Japan, Australia, England and Canada as well as the US. Several were with major research and development departments of large corporations such as DuPont, Virginia Electric, and the Army. We were all professionals in our creative fields of writing, enginering, marketing and manufacturing. There were several more men than women. I understood immediately that this was not a casual metaphysical workshop.

After our facilitators concluded the orientation, Denis, the one who organized the search for my keys, made an announcement.

"For those of you who are not already aware, Claudia has lost her set of car keys, There are several keys on a big purple clip. While we are out and about, let's be on the lookout for them."

I stood and thanked everyone for any help they could give.

The workshop prepared us to alter consciousness through the Hemi-sync sound process piped into our CHEC units during each session. The out of body experience was actually secondary to the real purpose of the institute. The main focus was to perfect a participant's ability to expand and access higher states of consciousness. We were actually participating in the research being done at TMI. I found it very exciting to be a part of it.

I know that the corporate participants were there to learn to access more of right brain creativity. I began to realize that the reason I was there was to raise my vibration to a higher level. I was fine tuning myself, expanding consciousness yet again, the central theme of my life.

For the duration of the six day workshop the disappearance of my keys became the subject of many jokes and pranks. Perhaps the importance of the fun and jokes around the keys helped draw us all together. We became very comfortable with one another and were able to share our individual experiences with the Hemi-sync sessions easily, some of which were very personal. We were, after all, probing deeply into realms of consciousness previously unexplored.

It did not matter where we were in our exploration of consciousness. We each brought something personal back to share if we so chose. That we felt totally comfortable sharing was a measure of how successful our facilitators and the Institute itself were in creating a safe sharing environment. It is a wonderfully freeing feeling to be able to talk openly about spiritual and emotional experiences as well as experiences of other dimensions of reality without fear of ridicule.

Robert Monroe came to speak with us one of the evenings. He and his family lived up the hill from the institute, overlooking the valley. He was a charismatic character and a brilliant storyteller. He was so at home with himself and his audience he made us feel that each of us was an old and dear friend. I particularly enjoyed his lively sense of fun. I loved the smile and mischief in his eyes. He brought his amazing adventures out of body to life and had us riveted for the evening. He answered our endless questions with humor and patience.

He shared that he was working on another book and even asked for our opinions regarding certain aspects of it. Since he continued to explore out of body he had an endless field of research from which to draw. He was crafting another workshop from his outline of the forthcoming book. We were thrilled to be included. We would have kept him there all night.

I count myself one of the very privileged to have spent time with Bob Monroe. He always remembered me on my subsequence workshops and stopped to share and catch up on the latest. He had this pleasant, comfortable way with everyone. It was this personable approach that made him a successful person in all his endeavors. And it is his vision and spirit that inspires the institute to this day.

The Gateway program was scheduled for mornings and afternoons with a 2 hour break at lunch time. We were free to explore, swim in the lake or just hang out. I loved walking the hills and soaking up the energy of the valley. There were several small farms in the area as well as many artisans inspired by the peace and beauty that surrounded them.

About mid way through the week we were encouraged to try for an OBE. The Hemi-sync sounds we were listening to were preparing us for such an event. We could start small and gradually evolve to the ultimate escape from our corporeal forms.

As I was falling asleep the third night I decided to try an OBE. I gave myself permission to go with it but after several attempts I could not get away from my physical form. Finally giving it up, I rolled to my right side to go to sleep but was startled to have only my astral body roll over. I could feel both my physical and non physical bodies. My physical body was stretched out flat on its back and the nonphysical body was on its side. I tested this by rolling back into my physical body and rolling over to my left side. My consciousness seemed to be intact and functioning well. My physical body was awake but totally relaxed on its back. I finally got bored with just rolling from side to side and went to sleep. I thought it was not a bad first effort.

During a session the following day, I made my first attempt at a controlled OBE. I turned up the sounds being piped into my CHEC Unit and settled down for whatever would happen.

I decided I would play it safe and just take a walk around the building. To leave my body, I imagined floating up and out of it. That didn't work, so I tried a deep breath and exhaled through my solar plexus. Perhaps, because I had proven to myself the previous night how comfortable and easy it was, I lifted right out. I left the room, not walking, not floating but seemed to have my feet on the floor, though I could not see them. I couldn't see any of my body but could sense its form. I moved with ease.

Looking around the hall, I found everyone else in astral form, standing in line for the bathrooms! *Even in astral form?* I thought. This struck me so funny I returned to physical form laughing out loud.

I could hardly wait to get to the group to ask if anyone else had that same experience. No one did, but I assured them that their astral bodies were there, all lined up, and I had conversed with a couple of them. We found this very amusing. Many thought that since we spent so much time lined up at the bathrooms that we left an indelible ethereal imprint there.

My next time "out" I lifted to the roof of the building and found everyone was already out there. I could see them clearly, sitting on the roof, chatting. I asked if we were holding class up there. One of the facilitators was present. Nothing much was going on; just chit chat. I remember thinking how uneventful and pointless the trip was. Why would I want to spend time hanging out on the roof? I did own that I was a bit reluctant to try to go further with exploration on my own. Truthfully, I was a little afraid I might create a negative experience.

No one else in the group had experienced a shared OBE. And no one had done anything extraordinary while out of body. We all seemed disinclined to leave the nest.

Then finally the evening set aside for the ultimate OBE was upon us and we all agreed that it was do or die. I was determined to do something more than just hang around the facility. Our coaches impressed upon us that our intent was very important along with the ability to feel comfortable with the experience. Fear could keep us locked in the physical. The Hemi-sync sounds piped into the headphones of each CHEC unit were set for maximum lift off.

Performance anxiety had me trapped in the physical for some time until I talked myself down to a more relaxed state. I asked Phil for help and gave a mighty breath push from my solar plexus. I shot right out and up into the night sky. Whoa! It was exhilarating. Fun! I did a few turns to see if I had any control over how my astral body performed. It was actually easy. I could execute any action I wanted to but understood that my expanded consciousness, through will or intent, was the one in charge. My brain or mind felt like business as usual. Just the body had shed its physical form.

I performed a few flips and a couple of tuck and rolls. As I felt more comfortable I tried some of the complicated high board competitive dives. I congratulated myself on my perfect 10 form. I couldn't actually see my astral body though I could feel it. It felt delicious, loose and free. I could clearly see the astral forms of my classmates. Many of us were out there cavorting about with abandon.

The ultimate experience for me was my flight as a hawk. After my Olympic dives I imagined myself a great bird of prey. I wanted to get the feel of the speed of the hawk as it swoops and dives through the air. All it took was the thought and I was zipping through the mountains instantaneously. Though it was night I had perfect vision. Everything stood out in colorful relief. If this was what those birds experience every day I'm coming back next life as one of those glorious creatures. I was ready to spend the rest of the night in the air. It never occurred to me to go visiting family and friends as some of the group did. I was having too much fun flying.

I don't remember making the decision to return. I just know that my bladder was full and needed attention. I came back to my body pretty fast and had to jump up and run to the bathroom. The relaxation required for OBEs is a double edged sword. I made a mental note to myself not to take in a lot of liquid before the next flight.

Some of us had OBEs where we were all together, though none of us had the same experience. The facilitators could not explain why we could see each other but not share the exact same experience. Perhaps we just felt safer in our group and thus created that for ourselves. I don't remember if Bob Monroe had anything to say about this in any of his books. Perhaps someone has the answer to that question.

Some of the class were unsure that their experiences were actually OBEs and not a dream. My dreams are very different from OBEs. I have way more control over my actions in an OBE. I can feel my body though I may not actually see it. My thoughts are clear and clearly mine. In my dreams I am usually an observer. In OBEs I am a participant. And the landscape makes more sense. Nothing seems muddled or cloudy like it can in a dream. Visibility is crystal clear.

To get to the actual release from my physical body with a controlled OBE, I have to cast or catapult my astral form with strong intent and a hardy breath. I usually come out my solar plexus first as if I were in an exaggerated backward swan dive. That just may be my need for elegance. I don't remember ever seeing a silver or gold cord attached to my physical form that some have reported. It might be considered a safety cord, a way back, as it were. I believe that we have so much freedom here in time/space reality we can create anything that makes us comfortable. My favorite Robert Monroe quote is, "The greatest illusion is that mankind has limitations." There is no place on earth to better drive this point home than TMI.

All through the week, I would check to see if my keys had turned up anywhere. I kept looking in my bag expecting them to be there, but no such luck. I finally had to call a friend in Connecticut to Fed-Ex a second set so I could get home.

My alternate set of keys had arrived the afternoon before our departure date. Two members of the workshop had waylaid me outside my room and asked to see the keys. When I showed them the second set, they grabbed the keys, put them in the palm of my left hand and wrapped layer after layer of masking tape around them until it looked like I had a club attached to the end of my arm.

"We just want to make sure that you don't lose these," they explained.

They thoughtfully left my right hand free to manage stuffing my face. You cannot imagine how hungry you can get doing work in consciousness. After each session we all would descend on the table the staff had set up with fruit, nuts and yogurt. But no one gained a pound!

I was going to miss these people. The sense of fun that Bob Monroe embodied was contagious in the personnel and participants as well..

The workshop officially ended with a recap of the week after dinner. We were due to depart after breakfast the following morning. Our facilitators returned our watches but no one wanted to wear one. No one wanted to leave the group so we sat around talking until we couldn't keep awake any longer. Bets were made to see if the second set of keys would still be in my hand after the tape was removed. They were.

Our last morning together we all were busy getting ready to leave. Before I packed my bag I gave one last thorough look for those confounded keys. One of the TMI associates assured me the keys would be mailed to me when they were found. I thanked her and went to stash my belongings in the car.

Approaching, I was amazed to see the windows were down and when I tried the door I found it unlocked. *What is going on?*

The interior of the car was a little damp from being open to early morning condensation. How many days had my car sat unlocked with its windows down? It appeared to have been restored to the way I remembered leaving it six days before. The pen was there in the cup holder. The whole situation was just mystifying. The doors were locked and the windows were up for the duration of the workshop. We all walked past my car several times every day. Surely someone would have noticed.

I climbed in the car, after wiping off its wet seat and sat for a minute gripping the steering wheel. *Am I losing my only mind?*

Driving home on the interstate, I noticed that cars where just zooming past me at disturbing rates of speed. I was in a peaceful, if somewhat bewildered, space, traveling at a fast but comfortable speed to get me home at a reasonable hour. I wondered why everyone was in such a hurry. When I looked down at my speedometer I saw that I was tooling along at 40 miles an hour, minimum speed for the interstate. *Maybe I should just put my watch back on.*

When I arrived at my house, I dropped my bag at the front door and heard something clink inside it. I unzipped the side pocket and was dumbfounded by what I saw. The keys... the keys that were so large a set that they made a bulge in the side pocket... easily discernable, impossible to miss. They made enough noise to have been discovered even while I was putting the bag in my car back at Monroe.

"Was that proof enough for you?" Phil asked.

Pardon me, I'm just going to stand here and scream for a little while.

I had asked for proof that I wasn't just playing games with my head. But even then I wasn't ready to believe those keys had just dropped into another dimension, or I had. I rushed to the phone and called two members of the class I knew would have made it home by then and made them swear they had not fooled with the keys. One said that without watches and being so focused in expanded consciousness it was not such a stretch to believe we were all in another dimension. *Oh well, the magic of TMI.*

Before I left for Virginia I had bought a lottery ticket for several advanced draws. When I checked the numbers a couple of days later I discovered I had won almost $2000; enough to pay for the workshop.

So the deal I made with Phil was fulfilled in every way. I was accepted for the August workshop, the expenses were covered by the lottery winnings and my set of keys provided the "key" to proving I was not just another air head. I am never without awe as I continue to experience time/space reality. It truly is a trip. And many thanks to TMI for all the fun of it.

Chapter Twenty Two

Perhaps, because I am naturally interested in sound, that soundfull (sound related?) events find their way into my life. I naturally attract them; which is the way of things if we stop to consider it or if we are paying attention.

I had picked up another book in my cozy book store where I had been unable to NOT buy Robert Monore's book. (But you already know that story.) This one was written by a California cardiologist, Brugh Joy. His book, Joy's Way, told about his spiritual awakening and how it had redirected and changed his life.

The following spring I was delighted to come across an advertisement for a weekend workshop being given by Dr. Joy on the effect of high intensity sound on altered states of consciousness. It was scheduled a couple of towns up the road from me at an old campsite for our local scouts. It offered pretty basic accommodations but I was up for it in order to meet Dr. Joy. I called my friend, Inger Marie, to see if she wanted to go with me.

We arrived, settled into the girls side of the bunk house and trouped over to the big gathering room. It was the typical wood paneled, screened room with an enormous fieldstone fireplace in the middle of the long wall. The kitchen and dining facilities were at one end and the gathering area for us was at the opposite end. What had been added to the room was four, sixty by thirty six inch speakers or amplifiers on the outer perimeter of the floor space. I could only imagine how highly intensive the sound was to be from those enormous speakers.

We were a group of 50 plus women and men. Inger Marie and I saw a couple of familiar faces and greeted them. People were gathered in small groups where lively conversation was beginning to raise the noise level considerably. My friend and I found a space, comfortably away for those giant speakers and put down our mats and pillows. I figured most of us would be listening to the music and sounds while in repose.

Dr. Joy stepped in front of the group and introduced himself. He was a good looking, trim and fit man somewhere in middle age. He was dressed in jeans and a leather jacket I would have killed for. He shared how he came to be there with us and what he hoped to facilitate in achieving altered states of consciousness with high intensity sound. He outlined how he would present the sound sessions. He would provide the music and the decibels. How we reacted or responded to the sound was for our personal experience. There would be discussion after each session. He cautioned us to be mindful and respectful of our bodies and ears and how much sound we could comfortably stand. He had chosen music that he figured would not be easily recognized so that it did not bring up associated memories, whether pleasant or not.

He invited us to get comfortable and with great anticipation, we grabbed our pillows and put ourselves in a relaxed state. The music selected was unknown to me but very melodic. It started softly at first and gradually got louder and louder. I made notice that the piece lacked an insistent percussive beat, but never the less, seemed to fill my head and chest.

There was enthusiastic discussion afterward. Many participants had some interesting experiences, The only noticeable difference I found for myself was an energy opening in my heart chakra; rather like someone in my chest knocking to get out. I found it rather pleasant. In fact the whole day was very relaxing and enjoyable.

At the end of the day and several music/sound sessions later, Inger Marie and I strolled back over to the bunk house and decided on sight that we could not stay there. The place looked like it had been invaded by a troupe of rowdy kids with clothes and gear everywhere. We grabbed our stuff and set out to find local accommodations for the rest of the workshop. Besides, we found ourselves ravenously hungry and were determined to find a good restaurant.

We were able to secure a comfy room at a small motel close by the camp and with a good meal tucked away, returned to our room ready for more discussion on the effects of the intensive sounds.

As we sat facing each other from our beds, deep in discussion, I began to notice a thin swirl of blue coming from my friend's head. She was into an explanation of one of her sound experiences and I was in my relaxed state, listening. While she held forth, I became intrigued by this blue energy emanating from around her crown chakra. I thought it probably was part of her aura. But looking at it started to interfere with what she was telling me. Funny that I could not listen to her and watch the blue at the same time.

After a bit she stopped her explanation and asked, "Why do you keep blinking your eyes?"

"You have this very pretty blue energy swirling around your head and watching it is rather mesmerizing. I don't know what it is going to do next. So, if I want to hear what you are saying, I have to try to stop seeing your aura. I was trying to blink it away but that isn't working. Can you shut it off?"

Needless to say that kept us up long into the night. The only thing that shut down the blue aura was turning off the light when we went to sleep.

Next morning we both overslept and ended up foregoing breakfast in order to arrive on time at the workshop. We almost made it but arrived just as the first music session was getting under way. The only space left to throw down my mat and pillow was right in front of one of those mega speakers. So down I went, putting my back to the thing, hoping to survive the blast. I don't know where Inger Marie put herself; later to find she went to the back of the room.

Right off I recognized the music as the 1812 Overture as it began to rattle the windows. Those who know the 1812 will agree it is an inspirational and rousting piece of music. I was just waiting for the cannon fire to send me into orbit. Preparing myself and my ears, I took several deep breaths, allowing the music to pulsate into my body a little bit at a time as I could feel comfortable with it.

When at last the battle came to fruition, the first cannon fire threw me into a dimension where I found myself in a forest, dressed as a young Native American female. Standing there, all alone, alert, but not really frightened, I looked around for others of my tribe but saw no one. I then remembered I was on a spiritual quest.

From somewhere deep in the forest a black, female wolf emerged and stood facing me with commanding presence. She was all that represented wolf in the feminine. She was magnificent, sleek and black with piercing amber eyes.

Looking into her eyes I felt the brilliance of her energy burst deep within my heart chakra.

Can you take this love? she asked

Humbled by what she was offering me, I answered simply. *"Yes."*

I felt her love spread all through me and around me. It stole my breath. The strength of her intent was so compelling I felt myself disintegrate and merge with the forest and the message of Wolf.

This glorious creature told me everything; the "rightness" of the animal and human connection; the eternal truth of Gia and what we represent as stewards of Her; the beauty and integrity of life in all its forms. I was awed by her wisdom. I overflowed with her love.

Reforming, more than I had been but still the essence of that which I am, I accepted the black wolf as my totem.

There was so much more but I cannot remember it. What I did manage to bring back from the experience will be with me forever.

I reentered the physical plane just as the last explosion of cannon fire faded away. I was a soggy mess, and having just a bit of trouble catching my breath. I don't know how I presented myself while I was fully engaged in the experience. Someone nearby asked if I was okay. I was beyond okay. I was transformed.

My wolf encounter was so personal that I did not share it for years. I had to give up trying to analyze how I was thrust into a different dimension or who I was or had been or how real it actually was.

Phil said it was as real as I was willing to allow it to be.

"You know that there are many physical as well as non physical manifestations of us as an Infinite Being. We have told you to observe the Tree of Life and know that we are ALL of it, every leaf, every twig, the flowers, the fruit, the sap, the roots, ALL of it.

"We have the ability and knowing to be totally aware and involved in all of our aspects at the same instant. Think of it as one of those medieval tapestries that depict the history of battles and families. It's all there, all happening at once on the tapestry. It just depends on where you place your eye or your awareness as to what you see or experience at that precise moment. The rest of it is there for you to experience whenever you desire."

Epilogue

It has been years since I first threw open the doors to the higher realms of consciousness. In that time I have had the privilege of living a truly exceptional life, seeking to satisfy my curiosity regarding the creation of personal and global reality. I have worked with pioneers in the field of mind expansion. I have taught and been taught many of the esoteric laws of the nature of reality. I have had encounters with angels, fought demons, and met my future self aboard a spaceship from another dimension. If this sounds fantastic, I can assure you that it never stops being amazing to me. Life is a remarkable journey that knows no bounds if exploring is your thing. I'm here to tell you it is worth the trip.

We truly are multidimensional Beings expressing our creativity in ways we cannot begin to perceive with our physical consciousness, and across more dimensions than we are aware of. We have the option to live large or small, expanded or contracted. We can be loving Beings or evil Beings. We are all individualized aspects of the ONE, Who loves us no matter how we choose to express our creativity. Who could ask for more than that?

I knew from the beginning that I would want to share some of my personal, spiritual experiences at some point. I set down an accurate and very badly written account in the beginning, knowing I would need a memory jog. I had tried to make notes while I could still function as an objective observer, but as I reached expanded states of consciousness, the need to analyze became totally unimportant. Some of the experiences were so strong that I will carry them over to all my many aspects. Phil had told me that when I was ready to set down the account, I would have all the help I need, to just ask for it.

Evolving awareness has Mutiversal impact and gathers momentum as it expands. It is the way of Consciousness, to continue to grow and expand, always striving towards intentional union with the ONE. When anyone of us, either physical or nonphysical, reaches a state of spiritual longing, with purposeful intent, that energy soars out and attracts events, circumstances, knowledge, teachers to aid our journeys along the path.

Phil tells me that it is Source calling us home, and making the way clear.

The author has been a long time resident of South Florida while sharing time with Connecticut and Virginia. She retired her need to save the world to marry a Connecticut Yankee where she became an organic farmer and renewed her passion for horses and country living. Her excitement for creating a full and joyful life stems from years of meditating and a fearless exploration of physical and non physical realities.

The author welcomes sharing and questions through ccstoner@claudiasbooks.com